The Auto Racing Guide: The Complete Guide to Auto Racing as a Hobby

By

Kevin Katzenberg

The Auto Racing Guide: The Complete Guide to Auto Racing as a Hobby

ISBN-13:
978-0996210416 (Hogan Technologies LLC)

ISBN-10:
0996210415

Table of Contents

CHAPTER 5 56

TRUCKS, TRAILERS, AND HAULERS 56

CHAPTER 6 80

TOOLS AND EQUIPMENT 80

CHAPTER 7 93

Introduction

I'm sure at some point in your life you said, "I wish I knew then, what I know now!" That's exactly what was on my mind when I set out on the journey of writing this, my second book.

This is a brain dump of more than twenty-five plus years of working on, setting up, and getting race cars to tracks week after week. A task I've been getting paid to do for thirteen plus years and a task I did as a volunteer years before.

Along the way I picked up some time saving, money saving, and headache eliminating methods. And, this book is where I pass them all on to you.

This is written in a relaxed easy to read style so even if you're not an avid book worm, like I am, you still manage to pull out loads of information to save you time, money, and a bunch of hair pulling experiences and frustration.

While starting to gather all the information together to put into this book, it feels like I've been through it all.

- Break downs on the side of the road.
- Wrecked race cars that need to get fixed to go back racing in the narrowest window of time.
- Frustrating motor problems.
- Even more frustrating handling problems.
- Setting up new shops to work on cars.
- Teams on tight budgets needing to compete with teams that have four times the money to spend.
- Finding and training crew members.
- Pulling all-nighters to get ready to race the following day.

Really, if racing grabs a hold of you, like it did to me, you will go through many of these same scenarios.

Here is the good news.
I have found solutions to many of the problems you will encounter.

I've brain dumped them, in a very organized manner, inside the pages of this book.

Many of the solutions I provide are not car or class specific. They will work whether you want to race dirt or asphalt, modified or late model, hobby stock or four cylinder, open wheel or fender car, and even road course or circle track.

If it has tires and a motor, most of the problems will be the same.

Here is a <u>brief</u> list of what I've put together and you will learn inside.

- How to figure out your budget and make sure you get the best equipment to win races right from the start.
- How to pick the right tow vehicle for your type of racing and separate the junk from the gems.
- How to set up a well-equipped shop but not break the budget with frivolous over kill.
- Basic maintenance items to keep your car running in top shape week after week; things I've learned along the way to look out for; even some little maintenance tricks to make your life easier.
- What I've learned about motors and their builders; how to choose them both and what to be aware of when shopping around.
- Where to find the best advice to get you running at the front of the pack.
- How to keep the family happy and maintain the perfect racing to home life balance.
- Finding crew members and keeping them happy.
- What kind of tools are mandatory, what tools are 'nice to haves', and how to get by on a limited budget.

- The best ways to get up to speed when just starting out or, if you're struggling, a way to get back on track.

I also have an extensive section on handling and drivability. (my specialty)

These are not a bunch of tricks and hocus pocus, but a solid foundation to help your racing adventure start on the right foot.

You'll learn:

- What is caster and camber and how you can adjust it to get the most speed out of your car.
- The most over looked and misunderstood front end adjustment which can add tons of speed and traction to your car.
- Having your tires point in slightly different directions can actually make you run faster.
- Checking your wheel alignment and why it is so important to the speed of your car.
- What is a panhard bar and how to adjust it to make handling changes. (It actually doesn't work how most people will tell you it does)
- Getting your head around weight placement and weight transfer; knowing this simple concept will put you years ahead of most of your competition.
- What is wedge and how to adjust it to get smooth fast car.

- Why I won't recommend using electronic wheel scales and how to figure out all your percentages with a calculator.
- How slip ratio and slip angle works to give you the most traction possible.

… And much, much more.

Here is how to get the most out of this book.

Only red the particular area you need help with at the time.

Skip around.

It is not necessary to read the entire book like it is a novel. I've tried hard to lay it out in a manner to be an easy to use guide to make your racing easier and more fun.

Each individual chapter is broken down into subsections or subchapters. These section headings are in large bold text so you can't miss them.

If you need help in any particular area, go to that area; skip the rest.

I also have a mailing list set up on my website to alert you of updates, new information, or just any information I run across that I want to pass along.

To sign up go to http://hogantechnologies.com.

Thanks,

Kevin

Now, as they say, "On with the Show."

Chapter 1

Getting the Right Racing Mindset

Getting into racing is quite the endeavor.

You will want to know and understand your racing mindset going into this endeavor.

This will ultimately set up what your entire racing operation will look like. It determines your budget, what class of car you will race, where you will race, etc.

The first question is, "Why do you want to race a car?"

Maybe it is a lifelong dream. Maybe you have a friend or relative who is already into racing and you are starting to get the itch.

Maybe on a whim you saw an advertisement, went and saw a race, and got interested enough to look into doing it yourself.

Maybe you are already involved on a crew and you really want to drive.

Racing is a ton of work to be successful.

Knowing your 'why' will give you the motivation when times get tough.

Having a strong why can also help you land financial support and find good crew members that will keep going when times get tough.

Having a strong 'why' is contagious. People will follow and may even push harder to keep you on the path to winning.

That is the goal, right?

If you a going to race, race to win!

It's nice to go and spend time at the track, but sponsors, crew members, and even family often times will have better things to do than go to the track every week. Having a strong why and setting good goals will keep everybody involved and pushing toward that common goal.

Racing as a Hobby

To tell the truth most of the people racing at even your most basic levels treat racing as more of a life style than a hobby.

This is many times something they have always wanted to do since they were a kid. And, it is a natural progression to start it as a hobby when they got older.

These types of people always keep track of what is going on at different tracks or in different types of racing.

If they get rained out for a night, they are usually headed to another track to race. Or, will go to a different track just to watch. But, they will always be with their racing friends where they will spend hours discussing racing.

It's a way of life.

Unfortunately, racing takes up such an intense amount of time and effort to be competitive, enjoying it strictly as a 'once in a while' hobby, will be difficult.

The learning curve is too high to just casually walk in and be competitive. Then later, after the races, put it way to the next race.

With other hobbies, you can put it away and not think about it until the next time you want to do it.

But, not racing.

With racing, it's much different. If you are in it to win, you will need to spend time figuring it out. Working on the car to get fast and keep it fast.

I recently talked to a racer who had been out of it for a while and decided to get back in.

After about two months over the winter preparing everything he needed to go racing, he remarked to me he forgot how much time needed to be spent getting everything ready.

He told me it was like another full-time job.

And, he only had to prepare the basics.

He bought a winning race car 'turnkey; ready to go'.

If he would have had to put the car together as well as everything else, he might have been burned out before the season even started. I've always said racing takes one of two things; time and/or money.

Money can substitute for time because you can pay people to put in the time for you.

But, you'll never substitute the time needed to be spent.

This kind of leads us into to our next topic.

Racing at a core level.

Why Race a Car

Years ago racing was filled with dare devils wanting to go fast and throw caution to the wind. The sport was dangerous and primitive. These were throttle stompers who smiled in the face danger.

Few rules governed the sport back then. Back yard tinkerers and hot rodders took to organized racing as a way to blow off some steam. They matched wit and skill against other back yard tinkerers.

They cut, welded, bent, bowed, drilled, and straightened their ideas into even faster cars. They smiled like a sly cat as they drove their latest creations through the pit gate.

Through the years racing evolved into rules committees creating complex rules to stifle creativity. Now a complete industry is ready to pump out any part for your car. Race tracks and sanctioning bodies try to create a business out of racing.

Every aspect of racing has become infused with money and it has become, unfortunately, a sport of dollars rather than a sport of thinkers.

I'm not saying pure creativity is dead in the sport, but creativity to make your car faster is now packaged up and sold to anyone who can afford it. Sanctioning bodies have now started creating rules that require you to buy rather than create the cars and parts to compete.

If you are the back-yard tinkerer looking to build his or her own creation and take it to the track and compete, you will need to find a class of car whose rules will allow you to do just that. This usually means sticking to the racing classes where the cars started life as a daily driver on the street.

A fair amount of creativity has been shut down on the full fabricated race cars. Any room left for creativity will be had at great expense.

The world of your higher end racing machines has been infiltrated with computers, design software, and vehicle dynamics software. As soon as one little edge is found, it is quickly outlawed in the name of keeping racing fair.

In the entry level classes at a track, the rules are usually a little wider open. You can get a little creative. Race tracks want the back gate full of cars. But, they don't want to pay a lot to have them there. This many times leads to classes where tracks are a little less tough on enforcing the rules. These are the classes where people get really good at concealing their cheats.

It cost money to enforce rules. Money to pay the inspectors for the time spent and equipment to do the more technical inspection.

The main thing they will be worried about is safety.

If you want to race a car because you are a dare devil wanting to cheat death every chance you get. The good news is that auto racing is still dangerous no matter how safe people try to make it.

People still get hurt and die unfortunately every year; even in amateur auto racing.

The sport has gotten a lot safer, but racer beware, bad things can still happen.

If thrill seeking through cheating death is not your thing and what you are really in it for is the competition, you are in luck.

Fierce competition waits for you in every aspect of the sport.

It's a game played well before you will ever strap your helmet on.

Strategy, cheating, brash trash talk, lying, disguising speed secrets on the car, and even maybe a little sabotage. Anything to throw you off your game and give the competition the edge.

Are you just wringing your hands in anticipation? Can't wait to get involved?

You'll be entering a world of intense strategy; not only on the track, but off.

A world where racers will continually try to woo inspectors and manipulate the rules to their favor. Beware of the subtle racer wanting to be a so called 'friend'.

When the helmet goes on and you hit the track there are no more friends.

If you relish hard core competition at every level you've come to the right place.

Tech inspectors can be swayed and promoters can be friended for special treatment. And, the trash talk begins long before you hit the back gate.

Racing is a chess game played by the drivers and crews which the average fan in the stands is often oblivious to.

Are you still with me?

Are you more interested than ever to strap in and get behind the wheel?

Let's look at some ways your mindset will determine how and where you will want to race.

Then will talk a little about budget and how to determine what you will spend.

Test Drive Before You Buy

One thing that is becoming more popular is testing the waters before you buy. You could rent time in a car at either a driving school or driver experience.

These usually aren't really expensive. I've seen them for $1,000 or less. I took one years ago for around $1,000, I think, which included one day of class in the shop and one day at the track.

Sometimes this is enough to get a little thrill and figure out it's really not for you without spending too much money.

Or, you might just get hungry for more.

This will go back to what you really want to get out of racing. Schools won't give you the thrill of competition. But, they can give you all the experiences of driving a car.

With the amount of work and time spent racing, if you rented a ride, went to a driving school, or checked out different driver experiences two to three times a year, you would be money ahead.

The other option is renting a ride. I've seen these in our area. You rent a complete ride for a particular night of racing. They bring the car to the track and work on it for you. You just get in an drive. These will give you the thrill of competition that schools or experiences won't.

You'd avoid a lot of headaches and many sleepless nights preparing for the upcoming races. Yet, you can have all the other competition experiences.

Where to Race

If you are just starting out I recommend staying close to home. If you don't have any current ties to the sport, investigate the tracks and the types of cars they race closest to you. Long commutes may seem ok in the beginning, but it will get tiring the further you get into the season.

Having ties to the sport will make your racing way easier.

In the beginning your tools and resources will be limited and it will be good to be around people you can get ideas or even borrow tools or spare parts.

It will help your learning curve a ton to have a mentor to park next to and give you advise or a hand along the way.

All the people I meet or I watch who start their racing career at the track I'm at, the ones who have a mentor or helping hand pick up on faster and do better their first year in racing.

Where you race will also be determined by the class of car you will race. I would not suggest racing a car that is out of your budget or skill level just because it is five minutes from your house as opposed to an hour.

It's better to travel an hour and stay within your budget than it is to spend rent money and race close to home.

I also think the opposite is true.

There are too many people who lay a social status on the expense of their race car. I shake my head at people who would rather travel hours away to race a class of car that is more expensive; just because of the social status it represents rather that the fun they will have.

If you can have just as much fun and get as much competition racing five minutes from the house with a more entry level car, why wouldn't you do it.

Besides, the whole cost of car reflecting the talent of a driver is B.S.

I know plenty of really good racers in less expensive classes of cars that can out drive much of the field in the more expensive car. There's no need to spend more and travel further if everything you need is closer to home and cheaper.

Let's Think About Budget

Now, probably the most important factor in determining how you will race is your budget.

Now, I'm going to be a little facetious here.

I heard a quote one time.

I think it was NASCAR driver Carl Edwards who said it. I hope I get it right here, but it sounds right to me.

How much should you spend on racing?

You should be able to pull your entire racing operation into the pits; and if everything burns to the ground ... truck, trailer, race car and everything ... and you can replace it, you are within your budget.

I would guess many don't operate within a budget like that.

Actually, I think most won't operate with a budget like that.

So, let's look at budgeting from a realistic point of view.

First, I can't emphasize this enough …

Don't race on food money, rent money, or retirement money.

Those are the big three no-no's.

Read it again and let it sink in deep.

As a matter of fact, I would suggest starting a separate checking account and start contributing to that account every paycheck; building it up a little even as you go through the decision and research process of your endeavor.

Take a certain amount of your income and put it away every month and see if you can live without it. You can adjust that amount as you go along until you get a stable amount you're comfortable with.

If you follow this rule, by the time you are ready to buy something, you will have a pretty good little nest egg saved up.

I cover costs of each individual aspect of racing in a little more detail in each specific section of the book. This should give you a pretty good way of creating your own ideal budget.

A Healthy Mindset About Racing

The first thing I will tell you; and, I guess, guarantee you.

You will never stop learning and experimenting if you want to get competitive and stay competitive in racing.

There will always be some new concept or part to try. Or, possibly something you see on someone's car that you believe to be the magic part.

One thing I've always done in racing and other things in life, as a matter of fact, is to strip everything down to a core level just to understand them.

From the very beginning of my involvement in racing I investigated everything I could at race cars. I dismantled them physically and mentally. I always looked for the core reason things worked the way they did.

This will help you separate the B.S. from the truth. And, believe me, the B.S. will get pretty deep in racing if you let it.

This way of thinking will help you make the correct decisions to get you the exact outcome you are looking for.

This will often times lead you down your own path; away from the unhealthy, monkey see monkey do crowd.

One time, I started comparing sprint cars to late models. A guy that had been around a while told me they are two totally different types of cars.

But, at the time I was looking at similarities between the two.

I thought if I could understand exactly what would make them similar I would understand the level of importance each change would make.

The same thing goes between asphalt and dirt cars. Even though they appear to be very different, they are actually more alike than you think.

To sum up the point I'm trying to make. You will be much better off looking at race cars from a basic level and ask yourself "why" people are doing things rather than looking at just "what" they are doing.

You will start to look past the gimmicks and tricks. You will have a more consistently fast race car. You will begin looking past the monkey see monkey do that plagues racing.

Sometimes people see something and chase it for months even though they know in the back of their head it is only just a mind trick; a diversion to what is really making someone else's car fast.

Don't get hung up on the diversions. Race your own car and don't worry as hard on what others are doing.

I don't mean ignore everyone else. Keep an eye on your competition. But, ask yourself, "How is that change helping their car and will that help me?"

Too many people rush into snap judgement changes because they see something on someone else car without understanding if it will actually make them faster.

Ok, let's start to look at what class of car is best for you to begin your racing career.

Chapter 2
Deciding What Class to Race

Some of you may have already chosen the class of car to race. Others may have a pretty good idea.

If you are at all on the fence or just want to race and have no idea, this section will help you decide.

I see too many people get in over their head on their first race car and it either takes such a financial or stressful toll on them, they end up quitting after a couple years.

That's why I always suggest you start out humble and simple; working your way up from there. Too many people end up with pie in the sky ambitions just to find out just how hard it is. And, end up trying to get rid of tons of equipment and tools for just pennies on the dollar.

Did I mention racing is not a very good investment avenue?

So, let's start off by figuring our budget.

Budget

In case you didn't read it in the previous chapter, I will retell it here again. And because I believe it is very important. To get in the correct mindset when setting the budget and choosing the car you will race.

I read something once that really resonated with me about a racing budget. I think it was in an interview with NASCAR star Carl Edwards.

If I remember it correctly, he said if you pull your entire racing operation into the pits and it burns to the ground, you should be able to stomach the loss.

It was something to that effect.

I like this because it says, don't race on money you don't have and can't afford to lose.

Racing can give you the highest of highs and the lowest of lows.

One minute you are winning a race and on top of the world. The next minute you crash and your car is a complete loss. There is no worse feeling than having your life savings tied up to something in the garage that is, basically, not worth too much after a bad crash.

I recommend for people who don't have a good grasp on what it will take to go racing is to start to set money aside before actually getting started.

Start modestly and set aside, say, two hundred dollars a week. With a very inexpensive race car, this should be close to getting you to and from the race track every week. (pit passes, gas, tires for your car, maintenance on your tow rig, etc.)

Every week add a little to that amount until you hit your threshold where your current lifestyle starts to suffer.

At this point you will have a number which you can endure every week.

Now, don't spend any of this money. Keep putting this aside every week while you search for and preparing to race your car.

By the time you are ready, you will have a pretty good nest egg saved up to get you started.

The biggest thing this does is prepare you to not have this money in your hand every week. If it's out of sight, it's out of mind.

I would even continue this practice through your entire racing career. A new big screen T.V. might look appealing in the offseason, but resist the temptation and build that up to put towards your car.

If you were racing this money would be gone.

The next thing you need to do is take stock in your startup costs. Prepare yourself. Take what you think it will cost and double it.
Ambition trumps clear headedness when you get the fever to go racing. Please keep the credit card in the wallet and plan your purchases shrewdly.

Too many racers always say they can get by with less, but in the end it actually costs them more.

You want to be at the top of your class for spending. It's a tough mindset to be in if you think you're not winning because you're being out spent. Know in your mind you have top notch equipment for your class and you can afford to maintain it.

A racer I helped for a while said it cost him five hundred dollars a week just to start the motor in his car. This was just to cover maintenance and freshening of his motor throughout the year.

This number didn't even take into account everything else he needed to spend to go racing. This just covered motor bills.

As you get closer to nailing down the class of car you can afford, begin putting together a budget for that particular car.

Figure things like motor freshening's, tires, possible crash repair, traveling expenses, gas for the race car (depending on the class of car you are racing, race gas can cost upwards of $10 a gallon), gas for the hauler, etc.

Is this number under the amount you are stashing away every week?

If it's over, start rethinking the class you are going to race.

Experience

This, it seems, is the next biggest trap I see racers fall into. The top class at your track may seem impressive, but these cars are usually very complicated to adjust and the competition is usually the toughest.

The people running these cars are very experienced racers with loads of time under their belt. I've seen too many people with stars in their eyes get swallowed up and end up quitting because they get in over their head.

Choose a class where you feel you can win at least one race your first season. You will probably need a spirit lifter some time in your first season. A win of some kind will help get you through the tougher times.

It's usually a good idea to volunteer on someone else's car before getting your own, just to see what is all involved with that type of car.

Remember you'll be learning how to drive as well as learning how to maintain and adjust your car. The learning curve can be tough at the tracks top end classes.

I always recommend to beginners that they choose a class without a lot of adjustments. Concentrate on keeping your car maintained and learning how to drive. It's more fun running at the front in a lower level class than going laps down in the top level class.

You can always move to a different class as your experience improves.

Location

Location seems to be the last big question I see racers struggle with when starting out.

I would suggest staying close to home in the beginning.

I cover this a little in the Trailer and Hauler section, but I should bring it up again here. Traveling to and from the races may seem fun at first, but hours spent on the road if you're not doing well, can get really old.

I always recommend staying close to home for your first couple of years even if this means not running a class of car which was your first choice.

This will also help on the budget side of things. It will be way cheaper and less stressful if you can be home within an hour of your final race.

When I first started racing, I really didn't follow any of these rules. I went in over my head in budget. I chose a class where I didn't have enough knowledge or experience to be competitive. And, since the class I chose to race was nowhere close to home, I ended up driving at least two hours every time I wanted to race.

I quickly got frustrated, was burned out, and went broke. It wasn't a fun experience. After pulling back from my own racing adventures, I decided to help other people and have studied and learned along the way.

I came up with this list from not only my own faults, but watching others fall into the same traps I did.

We all know the saying, 'if I'd known then, what I know now …'

This is why I'm writing this book. To help others not make the same mistakes I did.

Chapter 3

Getting Crew Help and Family Support

Racing is very time consuming and labor intensive. The more people you get involved or at least supportive of your new endeavor the better.

I know some people who go it alone, but most will need the support of family and friends to make it all work. Or, at least, make it somewhat enjoyable.

Support of Family

I heard one racer claim the highest divorce rate in the country was among racers and fire fighters. I'd have to check his statistics, but I know it will put a strain on relationships and families if everyone isn't at least comfortable with the idea of you owning a race car.

When beginning your racing endeavor, I would suggest sitting down with your family before you even start setting any other planning in motion and discuss the idea of you racing a car.

Some families may have time issues about racing, while others may have issues with safety. I would get them all out in the open before you get too far.

Do some research. (I hope this book will help you in that regard.)

I was lucky. I was into racing long before I met my wife. Her father was into racing before I met her. So, she was well aware of what kind of time commitment was involved.

And, she found out right away, I take racing way more serious than many do. I feel bad now, but racing became such an addiction, time with her often got put on the back burner to go to the races.

She does enjoy racing. Sometimes she would go along. Other times she would just give me a kiss and tell me to have a good time.

Kids can be a much more complex situation. This kind of delves into a parenting situation. Something I have no experience in and really shouldn't comment on.

But …

Some kids may get totally into it. Like me. Playing in the dirt in front of the grand stands with the other racing family kids.

Others may have serious issues with your safety. The thought of their parent being put into a dangerous situation may really terrify them.

In this situation, I would sit them down and explain some of the equipment you use to keep yourself safe.

I would even go as far as what you use in the garage when working on the car. Like jack stands, to keep the car stable when you are working on the car up in the air.

Some wives or girlfriends may need the same type of discussion. They may have hang ups with safety as well.

Racing is way safer than it has been in years past. Safety equipment keeps getting better. Information learned from crashes today lead the way to being safer tomorrow. But, there is always a possibility something can happen.

Time issues are something completely different.

You will most likely spend several days or evenings a week in the garage preparing for the racing. And, will often times spend a good portion of the weekend during racing season at the races.

Often times the off season will be as busy as during racing season.

There will time spent rebuilding and organizing. Repairing items on the car you really never had time to fix during the hectic racing season.

No matter how diligent you are with your race car, there will always be those things you just say "good enough, I'll get it done better later".

Later then comes in the offseason when your wife, girlfriend, or children are expecting for it to be done for the year.

The bottom line is to make sure everyone knows the extreme time commitment of racing. And, everyone is ok with it.

Crew Help and Friend Support

Unless you have the means to pay a crew, you will most likely have to rely on support from family or friends to work on the car.

If your crew is volunteer it is impossible to expect them to put in the time commitment you will.

Expecting too much will just wear them out quicker. Then, there will be more work for everyone else.

The work still needs to get done, but you'll just have less people to do it.

Most teams I know try to organize one night a week as a work night. Always try to be organized and know what you want to accomplish when people show up.

Disorganization and not being prepared to work are two of the biggest areas that can take a toll on crew members. It's pure frustration to work in a disorganized environment.

If you need to get parts, it might not be wise to organize crew days early in the week. Make sure you get all the parts you will need, so the job is easy to do. Make sure the car is washed and ready to work.

I hate working on cars that are dripping on me as I'm working on them, so I always try to leave a day or two between washing and working.

Or, even worse yet is working on a car which hasn't been washed at all. Make sure your car is clean and ready to go. Some teams I know split up the duties for what everyone wants to do or more by their capabilities and schedules.

The key to keeping a good crew sticking around is to make it fun for them. Many may say they don't mind working on a dripping wet mess of a car or crawling around on a wet concrete floor, but they are just trying to be nice.

There is one team I know which was some people show up on Monday to wash the car, then, others show up on Thursday and work on the car. The people who wash the like doing it and their schedules work out best to show up early in the week. The others hate washing and show up later in the week to get the maintenance and other work done.

Everyone gets something a little different out of working on other people's race cars. Some like the technical aspect. Learning how they work and finding solutions to problems.

Some like being part of the "scene". Just hanging out with friends and having good time is what it's all about.

But, I think everyone doesn't want it to feel like the grind. It shouldn't feel like they are going to work at their daily job.

Once the hobby becomes like a job you will start seeing crew help start dropping off.

Where to find help?

Working on race cars isn't for everyone. What you may find as you progress through your years in racing s that you will have one group of friends that will be your racing crew friends and other friends who won't want any part of it.

I've worked on many people's cars and have a ton of racing friends. Every time I watch someone get started in the sport, I see a particular pattern emerge.

Someone decides to buy a race car and they have a particular group of friends they hang around with on a regular basis.

They all decide to support the racing endeavor and want to help out on the crew.

Within the first couple of nights, or at least by the end of the season, all these guys are not around and an entirely new crew of people are helping out. It is a special type of friend who is willing to work for free and share your hobby with you. You will notice the difference as you spend more time in racing.

Most of these new group of people will most likely come from watching at the track and want to get involved. Or, they will be someone you met somehow through racing.

Auto parts stores, car shows, or just at the track, are probably some of the best places to find help for your car. If you concentrate on making your racing venture fun and stress free like a hobby should be, you'll be surprised how many people will gravitate naturally toward your racing.

Just don't ever expect your volunteer help to be as committed as you are. Be happy for what you get and thank them for everything they do.

There may also come a time when friends don't want to help out anymore. Maybe they start a family or just want to do different things with their time.

My advice is to wish them well and let them do what they want without holding a grudge. I think it's because racing is so labor intensive and so difficult that it's hard for a drive to see crew help leave.

I've seen too many drivers bash crew help because they no longer want to be around anymore. For a committed crew person and friend, it will be equally hard to leave. They will feel like they are letting down the team and it will be hard to let it go even though they really have no desire to come around anymore.

Like I said, the best advice I can give is let them go graciously. Still be friends and let them know it's ok if they want to stop by once in a while just to say 'hi'.

Who knows, maybe they will get the itch to do it again someday. Already having experience, they will be way more useful than someone who you will have to train from scratch.

Chapter 4
Finding a Garage or Storage

Now it's time to figure out what you are going to do for a garage or shop. It's always better if this is planned before the race car arrives, but sometimes you need to make do with what you have to work with.

When my boss got his first race car he really had no place to store it. He was young and just out of high school. He originally stored it at a buddies house. When his parents got mad, after a couple of months, he had to move it.

The story goes he actually had to move it several times that first year. He is a very successful racer, but what a headache it must have been constantly moving the car the first year he raced.

Going through all of that was really a testament to how bad he wanted to race.

My suggestion to you is to work out a good solution in the planning stages rather than during the racing stages.

In my mind, I divide the decision for housing a race car into two general categories. Either you race out of a home shop or you use something offsite.

The Home Shop

I consider a home shop something connected to or on the same property you live and own. Sometimes this is an out building.

Sometimes it is connected to your family's garage. Either way it is owned by you and it is within walking distance of your home.

Having a home shop can cause problems within the family, so I suggest before just moving the race car in, you have a sit down with other family members. Sit down with your family before even considering getting into racing.

First, consider whether your race car will be putting anyone out. Does your wife or husband park in the garage?

Are they ok with not parking in the garage?
Do you live in a cold snowy climate where not parking in the garage makes life a little more unpleasant?

They may say it is fine now, but look closely at your family. Try to read between the lines, so to speak. Could a move of your racing operation off site make things more pleasant for everyone?

If you are just dipping your toe into the water of this racing thing, maybe make an agreement that you keep the car in the family garage for the first year or two until you decide to take it further or that you have had your fill.

Let's think about some of the drawbacks of having a race car at your home.

First is the noise when you start your car. Usually this isn't too often, but if you have neighbors that aren't race friendly, even a couple times a month of running a loud motor may disrupt your neighborhood relations.

Another thing is the mess. Your car will need to be washed. Mud, oil, and even broken parts are a common factor to a race team.

Will your family want to look at and deal with the mess?

Will your neighbors be ok with the mess?

Do you live in a neighborhood that will be tolerant to the mess and noise of a racing operation?

Some communities have ordinances against certain types of vehicles parked in driveways. if your truck or trailer has lettering on it, you may be breaking one of the rules.

The bad thing is most of these ordinances won't get enforced until neighbors start to complain. By then you are all moved in and in race mode, when you will have to start dealing with the problems.

I would be a sleuth and do a little research about what you can and can't do in your neighborhood. You might even want to talk with your neighbors to let them know your intensions.

They may be ok with it, or say it will be fine as long as the neighborhood doesn't start looking like a junk yard. In that case, just be respectful of their wishes and keep your property neat and presentable. These people can make your life difficult if they want to, so it's usually best to work with them before problems escalate out of control.

The next thing you would want to make sure is that you have enough room. What may seem to be the ideal space when you are in the planning stages may end up being too small when all is said and done.

It always seems storage becomes a problem with any hobby I get involved with. I tell myself I'm only going to need this and keep it simple and compact. Sooner or later I run out of space because I've purchased more stuff to help me with my hobby than I originally intended.

Racing is no different. Plan ahead and leave yourself enough room so when you buy new tools or equipment you are not cramped.

There are some good things about storing your car at your home shop. The main thing is being close to your family.

When the works done for the day, it is easy to just shut the door to the shop and be close to your family. Or, sometimes family members may wander out into the garage just to see what you are doing. Kids could come out and say 'good night' before bed.

This could help bring the family together and closer to your venture. Resistant family members may warm up to the idea if they are around the race car all the time.

The other positive aspect is that after a long night of working on the car, it is really nice to just shut the door and go to bed. A long ride after working on the race car can get tiring.

Off Site Storage

This rolls me right into the other option for storing your race car. We'll call it off site storage.

This can either be renting something, using a friend's shop, or buying something out right just to house your race car. A couple of the same problems can arise as storing the car at home. Stuff like city ordinances, fussy neighbors, or running out of room can be a problem where ever you go.

The best solution would be to buy a piece of commercial property.

Commercial property is usually zoned and ordnance friendly enough to allow you to do everything you will need with your race car.

The problem is mainly expense. If you do dabble in real estate investing, this would be a no brainer. Find something, use it for your race car, then sell it or rent it out if you decide racing isn't for you.

Renting an industrial or commercial site to store your race car can get pricey. Also, I've never been a big fan of renting, especially if there is no return on your investment like running a business that can make you some extra money to help pay for the hobby.

The Racing CO-OP

I knew a group of people who used to share an industrial storage space. One person was a business owner who ran his business out of this space. He had enough room to allow a bunch of friends to rent out space in his shop to store their race cars.

I think there was around a total of six race cars all in the same building. Rent was reasonable. And, each person usually had one or two specialty tools that everyone shared. For example, one person owned a welder, another had a sheet metal brake, another had a lathe or a mill. It worked pretty well as a nice little community of racers.

There were occasionally some disagreements, but it functioned for close to ten or fifteen years without any problems.

They were all friends and they all trusted each other.

Trust is the biggest thing. As racing teams bring in new crew members, everyone has to remember that you are also bringing them into a shared environment. A good agreement needs to be had by all, before anything like this really gets off the ground.

In this case the business owner was the settler of any disputes amongst the racers. He was the final judge and jury.

This eventually fell apart. There were probably many reasons. But, mainly a lot of the racers quit racing and I think the business owner started expanding and needed more room.

If you know a group of friends, all with race cars, this may be something to consider.

Shop Extras

One thing that often gets overlooked is the number of extras that goes into a racing operation. If you are not running out of a home shop, things like water and electric are often taken for granted when looking at racing from a distance.

The truth is if you are working at a remote shop, the electric, water, and maybe heat, will have to be paid by someone. This could possibly be included into the borrowing of the space.

If you are fortunate enough to have the person letting you use the space also pay the utilities, that's great. What I see the most is that if you borrow a space to keep your car, it is still your obligation to pay the utilities.

For some reason these deals are often a handshake. A problem then arises with a difference in opinion as to who pays for the extras. I think it is best to take this into consideration upfront while making the agreement to keep your race car in the space.

If this is a space you will be renting, you will need to keep this in mind as an added expense for your rental.

Another Scenario

I have another friend who has set up a pretty cool racing operation for himself. He's been racing for years with a friend of his and is a pretty savvy business man.

He bought a small little garage as an investment property. It is in a good business location; i.e. tons of visible street traffic, in the right neighborhood, well laid out, etc.

He subdivided the building into two sections. The front he rents out to a local auto repair business. They get the good access, main street signage, and an office to run their operation.

The back is his to work on his race cars and other projects. They share an air compressor, heat, building security and other amenities. These amenities are things that make life easier for him working on his race car. They are also amenities he offers to his business customer.

If that auto repair business had to rent another location, they would have to spend extra to update that new shop themselves.

This also allows him to charge a little bit more for the rental portion. And, he gets the benefit also. He's worked out a pretty good situation.

Whatever scenario you decide on to store your racing operation, figuring it out before racing starts. It will save you headaches in the long run.

Chapter 5

Trucks, Trailers, and Haulers

Other than the car, the truck and trailer is what I concentrate on the most. I've been stranded too many times on the side of the road for hauler maintenance not to be on the top of my list.

Now, the truck and trailer see as much maintenance as the car.

Racing with a broken-down hauler is a head ache.

Let's run through some of the ins and outs of truck and trailer selection as well as what to maintain, and what areas always seem to be the biggest problem when trying to keep one on the road.

Budget

First, let's determine our budget and see what is absolutely necessary to get our car and crew to the track.

There is a saying in races that the hauler doesn't win the race. This is true, but a hauler can lose you the race, if you are broken down on the side of the road. Your chances of even racing get pretty slim when you spend time fixing your hauler on the way to the races.

The most important to any race hauler is reliability and generally the ability to do the job of getting the equipment to the track.

I know it's impressive when you see those big multi car haulers with full living quarters pull into the pit area. But, upkeep on those is a lot of work.

Everything on those things are bigger and heavier. They are tough to maneuver around tight places and are generally tougher to drive than a pick-up truck and an open trailer.

They have their good aspects as well. You can get out of the heat on a hot day without being cramped in a pick-up truck. They can haul more people if your crew is rather large. They have a ton of extra storage room for spare parts and equipment. And, many of them, have sleeping quarters to eliminate the needs for hotel rooms if you choose to race out of town.

New, those monstrous rigs will set you back several hundred thousand dollars. You can get them used for under a hundred thousand, but they will probably need some time and money before you start racing.

You might find a needle in a haystack. But, if one of those are selling cheap, there is probably a reason for it.

Bare Minimum Travel

If you're not raveling far, you don't need too much to get everything to the track. A simple pick-up truck with an open trailer will be a pretty good start.

I know people who have a two hour commute each way to get to the track who use an open trailer.

They are usually fairly in expensive, easy to maintain, and easy to store when not in use (if you've ever tried storing one of those large motor home multi car haulers, you know what I mean.)

The one very plausible argument I've heard against an open trailer is security.

Tools, equipment, spare tires, and spare parts are all locked safe and sound inside the trailer.

Many of the nicer open trailers have front storage compartments to keep everything secure, but the car remains out in the open. This also becomes a little issue if you get stuck in the rain.

What we've done in the past is take any seat padding out of the car (this usually just unsnaps) and cover the motor with some plastic to keep everything dry. Whatever you decide to cover the motor with, make sure you secure it well. I've lost many plastic bags and smaller tarps by not securing them well enough.

Also, make sure any ignition boxes or the distributor stay dry. It will be very frustrating driving through a rain storm only to get to the track and have your car not run. Ignitions hate water. Try hard to keep them dry.

It really depends on your comfort level when traveling. Going to the races and back on the same day, you really shouldn't have too many issues with security.

On overnight stays you might need to reconsider your comfort level with an open trailer. Years ago, we never had issues traveling with an open trailer.

Times have changed, and I'm not really sure if I would trust my equipment sitting out in the open while I'm sleeping away in a hotel room. I've seen more and more stories of people getting trucks and trailers stolen in recent years.

Years ago we never really thought this was an issue.

Types of Trailers

As you probably are aware, trailers come in all sorts of types and sizes.

They can range in price from under $1000 (used) to hundreds of thousands.

This is where you really need to keep your budget in check. It's easy get lured into something way beyond your budget and needs.

I mean, there is some really cool stuff out there.

This is the way I see the trailer market.

First, you'll need to make a decision whether you want to buy used or new.

There is a lot of really good used stuff out there. On the flip side though there is also a lot of junk. This goes for new as well as used. I've seen some new stuff that I just shake my head at.

Look up the manufacturer on the internet and look for some reviews of either satisfied or dissatisfied customers.

I'm going to give a slight caution to you about reviews.

You will always find someone who is unhappy with even the best products.

Then there are some people who take great pride and pleasure in writing negative reviews on products just for the simple fact of doing so. These may be perfectly fine, but some people take pleasure in trashing them. In internet land, we call these trolls.

Weigh the good with the bad and make your best judgement. If several people complain about one particular aspect, there may be a problem.

The biggest disparity in quality I find is in the enclosed trailer market.

These things are cheap and easy to build and there are a ton of people doing it. I'm talking about your 28' to 40' single car type of enclosed trailer. These are really easy to disguise with fancy options and all the cool racing stuff already built into the trailer.

Then after only a couple of years of towing, things start breaking and falling apart. I would always stick with trailers manufactured by well established companies that have been around a while. Chances are you will be able to find people who have used that brand of trailer. Ask them about their experiences.

Did it break down a lot?
Where there particular issues that kept coming up?

If they could change something in the trailer, what would it be?

Like I said there are a ton of companies who start up, build some trailers for four to five years, then go out of business. If you stick with a manufacturer who has been around for fifteen to thirty years you will have some idea they know how to build a trailer and you will have someone to call when you have problems.

Even having a place to buy parts when things break is a huge advantage when you want to go racing every week.

Many well-known manufacturers will have systems in place to get you parts you need on a timely fashion. They will have experience and channels set up ready to get you bulky large trailer parts right to your door.

When you need to get your trailer back rolling for the next weekend, you won't have time to wait for a call back while they figure out how to ship bulky trailer parts.

Most long-time manufactures have decent reputations and really want to keep you as a satisfied customer.

Having someone to call when you are in a pinch is a really good asset to have.

Then you have the real high end trailer market. These are usually the $100,000+ trailers with full workshops, multiple car carrying capacity, and maybe even living quarters.

If you are in this type of market, I will give you a couple pointers about what I know.

First, there is a choice between aluminum and steel built. Aluminum is lighter and easier to tow up and down the road, but will tend to wear out and fatigue faster. The only trailer manufacturer I am aware of who builds a quality high end aluminum trailer is Featherlite.

Then, there is the difference between aluminum and FRP walls. FRP stands for a fiberglass reinforced plywood. It is basically plywood with a smooth gel coat of fiberglass on the exterior.

This makes it very durable and eliminates the need to run steel or aluminum stringers up the walls to attach the exterior sheeting. You get a little extra inside clearance by using FRP because the entire wall is only ¾" thick or so, as opposed to the 1 ½" that is standard.

If you are running a class of car that is really wide, you might appreciate the extra room to get the car in and out.

The problem with FRP is can make a trailer a little heavier than standard construction.

You will need a hauler heavy duty enough and large enough to pull it.

If you are considering a trailer to carry two cars, you will need to consider layout. You can have a trailer where both cars fit on the bottom (this is usually a low ceiling trailer, an internal stacker (the car lift is inside and both cars ride one above the other), or a lift gate trailer (both cars fit nose to tail on the top with work space underneath).

If you are looking for a set up with lots of work space and storage, I would opt for the lift gate style trailer. A word of caution though, there are maintenance issues associated with lift gate trailers.

The ones that operate with screw jacks need to be kept clean and the screw jacks lubricated. If you race in a dirty environment, this may be an issue.

A hydraulic ram lift gate is your other option. These are a little less resistant to problems in dirty environments, but there are more parts to the system. These can have potential problems with pumps, rams or lines that can leak.

If you are considering an internal lift trailer, keep in mind the width of the car you are racing.

Just like choosing between FRP and standard walls, the internal lift will make the inside of the trailer narrower. If you are ever considering racing a class of car which is wide, I would recommend staying away from the internal lift trailers.

One thing you really should keep in mind is the carrying capacity of tires. You will more than likely need to carry some assortment of spare tires.

And, in some classes you might need to carry many tires of different sizes and compounds. Make sure the trailer you pick out has the carrying capacity for the tires you need to take along. I've actually tire carrying issues arise before.

A racer gets a great deal on a used trailer and actually forgets to consider what he needs to carry. He has problems like the car doesn't fit into the trailer, doesn't have enough storage for the parts he needs to carry, or doesn't have enough storage for the tires he needs to hold.

A great deal on a trailer doesn't end up being too great if it hinders your racing operation.

Let's look at some issues to watch out for if you choose to go the used trailer route.

Buying a Used Trailer

When looking at used stuff, give it a good look over and try to get an impression of the buyer and how he took care of his equipment.

If they are proud of their maintenance they will usually indicate it by telling you upfront about packing wheel bearings regularly, how new the tires are, or how recently they put brakes on it.

If they don't tell you, ask.

Other than tires, a lot of wear items can easily be concealed without pulling things apart.

Try to get an idea on how long they have had the trailer and how many miles might be on it. Is it a one owner trailer or has it been bought and sold several times.

Also, consider the reputation of the buyer.

Ask around the local racing scene. If you are buying it locally, ask people if they thought this seller took good care of his or her equipment.

I know a guy who is excellent at taking care of his equipment. And, I do not hesitate recommending people buy equipment from him. A good reputation and recommendation will go a long way.

There used to be several manufacturers of open car haulers with tire racks suitable for race cars. Now, since enclosed trailers have become so popular, these manufacturers have closed shop or started building enclosed stuff.

Here is another caveat to open race car haulers. Many of them are home built.

There is nothing wrong with home built trailers as long as they tow well, are reliable, and the parts they used to build them are fairly common.

I know a couple of people who bought trailers only to find out they couldn't even get spare wheels because the hub pattern the builder used wasn't a common trailer configuration.

Just finding a wheel so they could put a spare tire in the trailer became a huge problem. Make sure parts on home built trailers are readily available.

Take a good look at tire wear. If axles are out of alignment or the balance isn't quite right, it will usually show up in the tires as bad wear patterns.

If you can, try to see if you can hook it up to a truck and take it for a ride. It isn't real common for people to let you do it, but I have heard it being done.

With the trailer loaded or unloaded you don't want anything that sways or tows off center. Have someone follow behind you and watch it go down the road.

If the trailer appears to tow well, everything else can be fixed or updated. Make a list of the things that are wrong and use it as negotiating points when finally discussing price.

Trailer Maintenance

While we're on the subject of trailer mechanicals, I might as well give my list of maintenance items you will need to watch out for.

The first is wheel bearings.

I repack wheel bearings once a year on standard double axle open trailers. Unless you are putting on many miles, this should be sufficient. Some axles have an EZ-grease feature which allows you to put grease in the bearings with a grease gun without disassembling anything.

I'm not the biggest fan of these because it can lead to neglect. Manually repacking wheel bearings forces you to take them apart. If there is anything else wrong, you can usually catch it. The EZ-grease system lures you into a false sense of security that everything will be alright as long as you keep pumping grease into the hub.

One of the main aspects of taking it apart every year is to catch potential problems other than just lack of grease. Bent spindles, worn out bearings or failed grease seals are all potential problems that can be caught if the axles are taken apart regularly.

Oil bath hubs eliminate the problem of dealing with grease, but oil bath systems have problems of their own.

First, be careful not to overheat the hubs with the brakes or by putting wheel covers on which trap heat. Most trailer oil bath systems I have dealt with have plastic caps which can loosen with too much heat.

Too much heat can cause the caps to loosen and leak or just fall off all together. This causes the oil to run out and then bearing failure and catastrophic hub failure is soon to follow.

Another area to keep an eye on is the braking system.

I've seen all sorts, but the three most common are hydraulic surge, electric, and air. Air brakes are usually reserved for the larger motor home units. These are the most reliable, most heavy duty, and most expensive. To tow a trailer with air brakes you will need a truck equipped with air brakes as well. The truck will need to have an air compressor and an air tank system.

I don't have any experience with these, so I really can't give any useful tips. Just like everything else, probably get them serviced annually and if you feel anything unusual, get them checked out immediately.

Electric brakes, I feel, are the next most reliable on average sized race car trailers. They consist of an electro magnet attached to the axle.

When you step on the brakes it energizes the magnet. The magnet sticks to the inner hub face and actuates a cam system. The cam system swivels with the action of the hub motion and pushes the shoes against the drum.

It's fairly simple and straight forward. Magnets do wear out and get grooved and gouged on their face. As soon as the shoes show excessive wear or grooves, I replace them.

They are not real expensive. Most times it's best to replace them when everything is apart for the annual bearing checkup rather than waiting for them to fail.

Also, inspect the hub face. It will get grooved and gouged just like what can happen to the hub shoe surface. It's important this surface remains flat as well as the shoe area. To get good actuation of the brakes, the magnets need the ability to clamp firmly to the hub inner face. If the magnets get grooved, it can prevent proper clamping. When you need the most is not the time to figure out there may be a problem.

Broken wires or bad grounds are also common problems that can arise on electric brake systems. Wire brushing the grounding points, then spraying them with a special electrical protectant grease will help prevent corrosion.

Then last most common types of brakes are hydraulic surge. Located on the tongue of the trailer is a hydraulic master cylinder. As the vehicles applies the brakes, an actuator on the trailer tongue compresses the master cylinder and (just like car brakes) sends fluid to either the calipers or drum wheel cylinders on the trailer.

I'm not a real big fan of surge brakes because they seem to need constant maintenance to keep them working well. The most common problem I've seen is getting water in the system and it seizes up the master cylinder and or the calipers / wheel cylinders.

Trailers always seem to be the most neglected part of the race team, but when it's time to load up and go, the team expects everything to work flawlessly.

Surge brakes should be consistently bled out to keep the moisture out of the system. I think if you keep on top of them they might be ok, but most of the time there is so much other work to be done it usually ends up getting neglected.

The Truck or Hauler

Let's talk about the other half of the combo to get your stuff up and down the road. This will most likely be the more frustrating half filled with maintenance issues and expense.

This is the truck or hauler. There are a ton of different options available to you; ranging from the least expensive option being the simple pick-up truck or van to the ultra-expensive luxurious custom built race car hauler.

Let's start on the low end of things.

Pick-up Truck

I've seen just about everything you can imagine towing race cars to tracks. Up until a couple of years ago, a pick-up truck or van was the most common.

You can pick one up used pretty cheap. To tell you the truth, I don't think I would spend what dealerships want for a new one. These are basic tow vehicles to get your stuff to the track and to buy one new between $40,000 and $60,000, just wouldn't be worth the investment.

For what you can do with them and the limitations associated with them, they just aren't worth the money auto makers want for these new.

If you can afford to spend the $40,000 to $60,000 on one of these new, I would suggest finding something purpose built to tow your race car which is used.

I really should tell you up front that I do not ever finance a car. New cars are way over priced and depreciate to fast to be worth paying the interest rate on a loan.

Every car I buy is paid for in cash with money I have saved over time. Don't go into debt just to go racing, it isn't worth it.

The good things about a pick-up truck is they can be fairly fuel efficient (compared to other tow vehicles), easy to maintain, and fairly cheap to operate.

The down sides are that they don't have the passenger capacity or storage capacity other methods of transport have. You will have the bed of the pick-up to use for extra storage unless you get a goose neck trailer.

And, it doesn't have the towing capacity other vehicles have.

Let's stop and talk about towing capacity, and ability, for a minute.

Towing Capacity

I consider towing capacity to be the amount of weight a truck or hauler can reasonably pull without overloading either the chassis or motor.

Pick up's come in different configurations and are categorized by tonnage.

The capacity of a full-size pick-up starts at ½ ton; then goes to ¾ ton; then the largest being a 1 ton. This designation originated years ago when that was considered the carrying capacity of the truck.

I think by todays construction standards these numbers may be a little low.

For GM vehicles, these are designated by 1500 being the lightest duty (½ ton) going up to 2500 and finally 3500.

For Ford vehicles, the designation is 150, 250, 350.

A bare bones racing operation can get by with a ½ ton truck if you are hauling a lighter weight car, with a simple open trailer, with a limited number of tools or spare parts.

Myself, I'm usually over cautious. I don't like having problems and I really don't like being broken down on the road. I would stick with at least a ¾ ton capacity for even the simplest of racing operations.

Unless of course I live across the street from the track.

If you are just starting out racing and don't want the big commitment of a full-blown hauler, the pick-up truck is probably the vehicle for you. If you decide you don't like it after a year or two, these have tremendous resale value.

You will be able to resell this pretty easily.

What about a van?

The Van Possibility

They seem like a pretty cool option to the pick-up truck. You can hold more people and have a larger place to store your tools. This is absolutely true. But, there are a few things that I just don't like about a van.

First, a van large enough to tow a trailer can get rather expensive because they are a little harder to come by. These are usually designated in the same way as the pick-up truck. (½ ton, ¾ ton, 1 ton)

Again, I wouldn't go with anything under a ¾ ton. I've heard of people beefing up the rear springs to make them tow a little better, but I'm not sure if this helps.

Which leads me to the second point.

There seems to be a balance issue when you hook a trailer up to a van. I don't know if it is because the motor is moved back further than a pick-up, or what.

But, it seems any van I've ridden in with a race car hooked to the back always seemed to sag and sway when going down the road.

They just seemed to not tow very well.

I've know people who have towed with them and I see them regularly at the track.

I'm just not comfortable recommending them.

Now let's move up the ladder a little in terms of comfort and capacity.

Toterhomes

Let's talk about Toters, or Toterhomes as they are usually called.

Everyone has a different way of talking about the living quarter type of haulers.

I consider the toterhome to be a camper which has a platform on the back to accommodate a fifth wheel or goose neck type of trailer.

I then consider a motor coach hauler to be something with a tag trailer connection.

These also have their plusses and minuses.

They can have a much larger person carrying capacity, can usually pull more weight, and can have some nice amenities of home.

Some of these have kitchenettes with refrigerators, stoves, and microwaves.

Others have sleeping areas, full couches and tables.

Others can have bathrooms equipped with toilets showers and sinks.

Remember the general rule of thumb, the more amenities you have, the more there is to go wrong.

Especially if you are buying this stuff used.

The last team I helped bought a brand-new hauler. It was used heavily as a weekend racers hauler. We raced an average of two or three days a week. The truck never really got a ton of miles on it every year. We kept racing operations within a two or three state radius.

After about six years it started needing work. I'm not talking about just maintenance. Things would just stop working and need repair. Problems with the water pump, problems with the toilet, problems with the refrigerator, and so on and so on.

The repair on these things aren't particularly complicated, it just needs to be done.

With the work load of maintaining the car, you will need to make time, or have one of the crew members ready to keep the hauler maintained and ready to go down the road.

I see a lot of new racers with stars in their eyes watch those haulers pull into the pits.

They are impressive.

Be fair warned though that they are a lot of work to keep them going.

Chapter 6
Tools and Equipment

You don't need to spend a ton of money on tools and equipment when you are first starting out. But, there are some basic tools and equipment you will need either in the shop or at the track.

Your tool inventory will build over time. Trust me. Once you have been racing for a while you will always be consciously or unconsciously on the lookout for things to make life easier.

Basic Tools

First, you are going to need a basic set of hand tools. These are sockets, wrenches, a couple hammers, crescent wrenches, pliers, vise grip locking pliers, screw drivers, a punch and chisel set, Allen wrenches, side cutting pliers and channel lock types of pliers.

You probably don't need to spend a ton of money on these because frankly you are not making your living with your tools. You are using them with your hobby. Plus, the quality of the inexpensive tool lines has gotten much better over the years.

I get tools all the time from discount tool places like Harbor Freight because if you lose them or break them you don't feel so bad.

I do have a friend who is a Matco Tool dealer and there is a difference in quality. I love going to his shop and working with his tools because in some cases, it makes working much easier.

But, I'd hate to lose any of those wrenches at the track and have to replace them. (Trust me loosing wrenches at the track will happen. It's almost like it's just a part of racing.)

There are a couple of things I will spend a little more money on. I've noticed the quality difference between good and bad is actually hard to work around. The less expensive versions just don't cut it.

Ratchets

Ratchets are one thing I don't skimp on. When the ratcheting mechanism in the lower quality tools begins to act up, your frustration will escalate. They will either get jammed or only work in one direction.

It's really not worth the aggravation. I only buy the best quality more expensive quality ratchets.

Vise Grip Locking Pliers

On the cheaper brands the locking mechanism will not always work; especially after some use. The pivoting joints will begin to loosen up and they will start not locking. Or, they will not stay locked and spring open at the most inappropriate times.

Always get the Vise Grip brand and better yet, if you can pick up some older ones from rummage sales, I would go that route.

Vise Grips have changed over the years. The older ones are way better than the new ones. If you have some older ones, guard them with your life.

Channel Lock Pliers

When the pivot joint begins to loosen up, you'll feel like just throwing them in the garbage. I make sure and buy only quality in these also.

Channel Lock is a really quality brand, but Snap-On, Matco, and Mac also have really good quality in their tongue engrave pliers.

A couple of other notes on hand tools. It will depend on the class of car you are running as to what type of handfuls you will need.

If you are running an after-market custom build class of car in America, you will most likely need standard sized sets of wrenches and sockets. (½", ⅝", etc.)

If you are running a stock production class with a newer style of car, you will need a set of metric wrenches and sockets also. (8mm, 13mm, etc.)

GM started using metric hardware on their cars in the eighties. And, I believe all of the cars being run in the popular four cylinder classes now use all metric bolts.

As snarky experienced mechanics, may joke with beginners, no, you will not need to buy special metric crescent wrenches, metric Vise Grips, or metric Channel Locks.

Hammers

Your hammer may be one of the most useful tools you will get. I like a little variety here to match the different jobs on the car.

I like: A 10lb. sledge hammer or maul, large and small ball-peen hammers, a brass hammer to hit but not destroy things, and a plastic dead blow hammer or rubber mallet.

My hammer selection has branched out a bit, but this should a pretty good start.

Tire Wrenches

At bare minimum, you'll need some sort of tire iron or T-bar wrench to take tires off. Most aftermarket lug nuts are 1". This is what common wide five hubs and Grand National 5x5 hubs will have.

If you are running some sort of stock production class, those lug nuts may differ in size depending on what type of car you are running.

We use a ½" drive cordless impact wrench with a fancy socket just for tires. The socket is extended to reach inside wheels and the corners on the socket itself are rounded to help quick alignment on the lug nut.

The impact is nice and makes life easier, especially during pit stops. If you're on a tighter budget, I'd do without and go the T-bar route.

Air Compressor

An air compressor or some sort of air supply has become essential in racing. There is always something you need compressed air for.

When I first started helping out on a race car, we used to use an air tank at the races and the compressor stayed in the shop.

This is fine. But, I've seen too many instances where an air compressor is needed at the track. It's not essential, but it would be on the top of my list of things to buy when you begin to expand.

One thing I've seen people do is get cylinders of nitrogen to use at the track for compressed air. This can get pretty expensive unless you can land a sponsorship from a welding supply store.

The team I work for runs nitrogen gas charged shocks, so I always have a cylinder of nitrogen in the trailer just to keep the shocks charged.

But, we also have an air compressor that stays in the trailer do a basic supply of compressed air.

Some people swear by putting nitrogen in the tires to keep them from growing when they get hot.

This is a good idea if you are running classes and track conditions that see a lot of tire heat.

But, in our case, we just use air from the air compressor in our tires and have really had no problem.

Floor Jack and Jack Stands

Another essential basic you are going to need is the floor jack and jack stands. Back when I started in racing, the floor jacks where massive iron behemoths designed to strain backs and kill toes when dropped. They were also designed to lift cars, but that was an afterthought.

Mass manufacturing in china has led to the availability of lightweight aluminum versions. Although they are light weight and they look like the versions that they use in NASCAR, they are a far cry from it.

If you have a decent budget, I would defiantly recommend purchasing a higher priced professional jack like a Brunnhoelzl. The quality in these jacks will eliminate a ton of frustration in your racing. Although, I will say I would not blow the budget just to get one of these jacks.

A close second in my choice is one of the budget light weight versions from one of the discount tool sales stores. Or, one from the online retailer Amazon. The problem with these jacks are that the quality is not quite what it is from Brunnhoelzl.

You will probably buy two or three of these at least by the time you need to repair or rebuild one of the Brunnhoelzl jacks.

I would definitely opt for one of the cheaper lighter weight versions before I went with the old-style cast iron floor jacks.

These are ok if you are racing in a class where you need to lift a very heavy car, but I don't believe there are too many classes where you need something that heavy duty.

As a side note, you will need to keep an eye on the rating on the jack you want to buy and the weight of the car you want to race. They make a bunch of different sizes in the economy line of floor jacks. Make sure you pick one that will not only lift the weight, but get the height you are looking for. There are some jacks that are a little smaller and will not get the lift you are looking for.

As far as jack stands, I would make sure that what you buy has a large enough base to be stable. Many of the pit areas will be on uneven ground. Many times, standard jack stands will not be stable enough to use in the pits.

There are a bunch of companies that sell special designed racing stands that have a very large base to be stable on softer or uneven grounds.

In the old days, we used to get some standard production stands and weld larger plates to the bottom to make them more stable. Whatever you decide just make sure they are stable and will not sink into soft ground.

This is also true with the floor jack you choose. If you are going to use a floor jack in a dirt pit area, I would mount a larger base to the bottom to make it more stable. We call these dirt wings.

They make the floor jack wider so it is not so tippy. I don't know any actual statistics, but I would guess there are more people hurt in the pits from cars falling off jacks than any other form of injury.

Make sure you take precautions to keep yourself safe.

Battery Charger

The last main piece of equipment I think is absolutely necessary is a good battery charger. Many classes of cars don't run alternators because they can rob horsepower.

That means that to keep everything working power wise you will need to charge the battery manually.

Nothing too complicated here. Just get something well-made and reliable. It is sometimes nice to have the ability to use one with a 50amp boost mode. If you are having problems, you may need something with enough amps to turn the car over with the charger.

This not the recommended use of a battery charger, but when you are in a pinch and don't have time to let the battery charge, it is a nice option.

For normal use, just a standard 5-amp trickle charge is all that you will need.

If you are using a 16-volt battery, you will need a special 16-volt battery charger. Using a 12-volt charger can wreck the battery. Most of these chargers are electronic and will meter the charge depending on the condition of the battery.

Lighting

Lighting at the races is pretty much a given. Even if you race during the day, you will need some lighting to get some jobs done on the car.

At bare minimum, a couple flash lights are necessary. I also like to have a work flood light or mechanics drop light.

As far as type? I am everything LED. For their brightness and their energy efficiency, there is nothing better.

Nice to Haves

Now let's talk a little bit about some tools I would consider 'nice to haves'. These are tools that will make your job easier, but aren't necessary.

I've been around racing too long to go without these things. But, if the budget isn't there, these are the things I would without.

Generator

I think some people would put a generator in the category of 'must haves'. I've done without one in many circumstances, but it sure makes racing at the track a whole lot easier.

The sizes and prices of portable generators have come way down in recent years. A simple, small, hand held generator can be had for less than $500. Weighing in the benefit a generator can provide at the races, it's pretty affordable. And, if you use LED's you don't need much of a generator to provide the simplest of power.

I've been to tracks which have power for you to plug into. This was years ago and I doubt there are many tracks left which supply electric. I think people kind of abused the system.

If you've ever seen the Christmas Vacation movie where the plug outlet was overloaded with cords on top of cords with multiple power strips and three into one's, you know what I mean. It was a mess of maybe thirty cords plugged into one outlet.

That is what was happening at race tracks that supplied power for you to use. I can't believe there weren't more blown fuses or electrical problems than there were.

More and More Tools

As time goes on you will continually find more things to help make your job easier.

That's what tools do.

One thing to always keep in mind is how much easier it will make the job as opposed to the cost of buying the tool.

Chapter 7
Motors and Their Builders

Building motors and motor work, even at the most basic level, hasn't even been something I'm very fond of.

The team I work for now gets their motors pretty turnkey and ready to drop right into the car. This works great for me.

They come fresh off the dyno. All I need to do is drop them in, hook them up, and give then an initial startup to make sure everything runs as it should.

There is a little ritual I go through when starting every motor and we'll talk about that a little later along with some little tricks to make motor installs a little easier.

First though I want to talk about motor builders and some things to make sure you get the best deal you are paying for.

It's hard to tell exactly what you have when you buy a motor from someone. It is just sitting on the floor all sealed up. Usually they washed and any visible oil leaks or problems have probably been erased.

When these things are buttoned up and fancy, it is really up to the trustworthiness of the person you are buying it from as to what is inside.

This especially holds true if you are not a motor guy like me.

I've never been real trusting of motor builders. I've heard too many horror stories.

Although, in motor builders defense, I see many cases where they get a bad rap when things blow up and it wasn't their fault at all.

If you are buying a motor and you have a friend who knows motor parts just by looking at them, take them along.

I've heard some motor builders agreeing to pull the oil pan off so you can inspect it. Although, it is a rarity.

If you are completely new to the sport, I would do some research. Visit the track you are going to race at and look around at some of the popular motor brands.

See what is consistently winning. Usually there are two or three that will be prominent.

Every motor builder has their own combination they like to use. And, usually it is class specific. What is fast in late models might not be good for modifieds or hobby stocks.

I'd also look at turnaround time. Some motor builders are months behind. If you break a motor, it's nice to know that you can get a quick turn around and get back racing.

Depending on where you live, the season can get pretty short. Waiting for a motor rebuild can tear into quite a bit of the season.

Let's side step a little and I'll tell you a little about owning my own race car.

My budget was too low. I was racing on money I shouldn't have been spending on racing. Basically, doing the opposite of what I recommend in this book.

I broke a motor a little way into my first racing season. Without a reasonable budget, I struggled getting it fixed and back on the track. Just as I was learning and getting a feel for the car, I had to sit out.

When you are learning to race, time on the track is critical. That is why I stress racing within your means.

I swore after I quit racing because of lack of funds, I would never go racing again unless I could afford at least two motors.

Too much effort goes into every other aspect of racing to be side lined because of a motor failure you cannot get fixed before the next week.

Another really important aspect of choosing a motor builder is whether they are at the track or not. Many motor problems arise at the track. Having your motor builder there to help diagnose the problem will be a huge asset.

Many problems will be hard to describe when you are on the phone or in the garage. If you do not have a ton of experience with motors and searching for problems, it will be difficult and time consuming trying to iron them out.

It's often just easier for an experienced engine builder to just walk up to a running motor and know by the sound to look for the problems.

It might even be wiser to pay a little more for an engine knowing the builder or at very least a member of his staff will be at the track to help you out if you have a problem.

I also look at what a builder usually charges for rebuilds and what they consider should be the frequency for rebuilds.

Most motor builders will tend to have a number of laps or a number of nights they will want to get it back and go through it.

It's good to ask builders these questions up front before you buy something and the cost or frequency of rebuilds goes way beyond your budget.

I don't believe it's wrong for builders to expect frequent rebuilds or replace quite a few parts as a standard rebuild.

Look at it this way.

Motor builders are trying to build a reputation. If their engines are blowing up because of part failures, it makes them look bad. By insisting on more frequent or more expensive rebuilds, it helps them build their reputation of reliability.

Especially when part failures are something which is out of their control. They buy the parts from a third-party manufacturer and their only control is the decision to buy or not to buy.

Most times they have no control over the manufacturing process of the parts they are using.

Just hope they are upfront about rebuilds. If they tell you to have a motor freshened every five hundred laps. And, the motor blows at six hundred laps, you really can't blame the builder.

If the motor comes apart fifty laps in after an expensive rebuild, I would look for some reasons why.

Motor Basics

As I said motors are really not my thing. But, I do have some tips and advice for you to follow to hopefully alleviate some problems for you in the future.

First, advice I have is when putting your motor in the car. Alignment and time is your friend. Take your time and don't force things. Make sure everything lines up, if it doesn't do some investigation on why things won't go together.

I've seen people force things where something is not lining up and end up breaking parts by trying to pull it together with bolts. Just take some extra time and do a little more research why things aren't working.

Second, find out if there are any special requests by your motor builder for initial start-up.

One motor builder I know, insists on putting some sealer into the cooling system on initial start-up. Some motor builders may have no particular requests.

Here are a couple of things I do for every initial start-up.

I always check the timing. Even if your motor has been on a dyno, the timing mechanism might have gotten bumped on installation or travel from the builder. Checking the timing is just a simple way of making sure everything is right.

Check with your builder to make sure you know what they want the timing set at.

Some builders put a tag on the motor stating what the timing and valve lash should be.

After checking the timing, I top off the radiator. Running the motor will usually eliminate any air pockets left in the motor.

Here is another tip. Always make sure the radiator filler neck is the highest point when trying to get all the air out.

Sometimes the radiator is lower in the car to try and get the weight down or get the nose lower in the car. You might want to jack up the front of the car to raise the water filler and make it higher than the rest of the motor.

Then, I always check the level of the power steering reservoir. To prevent aeration of the fluid, I get the level above the return line port.

This will prevent the return oil from splashing air into the fluid.

Another area I spend extra time with is belt alignment. You will, more than likely, be turning your motor at more RPM than any street motor. I always recommend a good set of aftermarket pulleys.

Stock pulleys are ok for the lower RPM's of street motors, but aren't the best choice for higher RPM racing engines. And, always take the extra time necessary to make sure they are in perfect alignment. Bad alignment will lead to belts coming off and belts wearing out prematurely.

You will, over time, learn more and pick up some of your own rules of thumb or tricks. No matter how many motors I install, I always keep learning more.

Chapter 8
Weekly Preparation

I think one of the biggest and most overlooked aspects to going racing is budgeting time. Proper planning to getting everything done to go to the track every week is a must.

Here's the simple truth.

For a volunteer racing venture, you'll probably never get everything as perfect as want to go racing, week after week.

Some people will be better than others. The further involved you get, the more you will realize that like most things in life, your eyes will be bigger than your heart.

You'll hear people say, "you need to do this every week". You'll read a magazine article which will expose some super racers weekly maintenance check list. That checklist will be as thick as a dictionary and you feel in order to be successful, yours will need to be the same.

The honest truth is there is only so many hours in the day, and taking into consideration the size of your crew, so many hours in the week to get everything done.

Don't sweat it. Don't get worked up too much if your check list doesn't get totally completed every week.

Things may come up in your life. Things may come up in your crew member's life. Sometimes things just won't get done.

It happens to everyone.

If you are in this as a hobby, do what you can and at the end of the week, put a smile on your face, go to the track, and have some fun.

All that being said, I'm going to give you a quick run-down on what I think is important and I think is over exaggerated in the weekly preparation realm.

Making Sure It Won't Fall Apart

Making sure the thing won't fall apart is number one. If you've been around racing at all you've probably heard the old adage," To finish first, first you must finish!"

This is 100% true.

And, to add to it.

It will make racing not much fun, if every time you go to the track something is breaking. Then you spend all your time just keeping the thing running.

It makes for a long night if you need to keep working on the car.

The first thing to work on in the shop is your maintenance and making sure things will last the night.

A Bolt Run

The simple thing of making sure bolts are tight will save you hours of frustration and possibly some premature baldness. I know I've pulled my hair out many times when something so simple as a bolt falling out cost me many hours of work putting things back together.

Checking the bolts on your car won't take more than an hour and it will be probably the most important thing you will do on your car all week.

I suggest putting your car on jack stands, taking the tires off, getting all the wrenches you'll need, and go all the way around the car checking bolts.

Then get on a creeper, roll under the car and check the bottom side.

Here is a little secret.

After the first couple of weeks, you'll find patterns emerge. Some bolts loosen up every week and some you may need to tighten only once a month.

I use Nylock locknuts on every bolt I can. This will prevent much of the vibration loosening problems.

Usually, after I assemble a new car, I will need to go through and re-tighten everything at least twice after we start running it. After that, much of the car will stay tight week to week without having to re-tighten.

But, the first couple of weeks on a new car will loosen everything up.

Crash Repair

This should actually be at the top of the list, but some crash repair can actually be overlooked if you are in a pinch to get to the track.

The crash repair that is absolutely essentials suspension or steering damage. Or, anything that may prevent you from finishing the race.

If you hit the wall with the front end, make sure all of your suspension components are straight and your rack or steering box is ok.

If you hit the wall with the back end, make sure the rear differential and suspension is ok. Make sure the fuel cell isn't damaged and all the fuel fittings are ok. Sometimes fuel fittings can get bent and cracked and not show a leak until the car starts to run again.

If your battery is in the back, make sure it isn't damaged and all the terminals aren't rubbing against any interior panels.

Steering Gears

Sometimes steering boxes or racks can get damaged internally and you'll never see the problem until you go and hit the track the next week.

I'll always steer the car back and forth without the motor running. If you do this without any load on the front tires (with the car on jack stands) you can usually feel any anomalies in the front suspension.

Steering should be smooth. If you think you feel any bind go through and investigate it further.

Sometime you can chip a tooth on a rack or box and you'll never feel it with the motor running because the power assist will overcome the problem.

Once a tooth starts to fail, it will only get worse over time.

Also, bent rack shafts can be a problem. If you even think you have a problem, disconnect the tie rods from the rack and continue running it back and forth without the motor running.

It will feel like a hard spot as you steer.

Fluid in the system may make it difficult to detect potential problems.

Without the motor running you will be trying to push oil backwards through the system.

Drain the fluid from the system and disconnect the lines and continue to run it back and forth. Put some drain pans under the car because this will make a mess.

Oil will come squirting out like a fountain as you steer several times back and forth. Eventually, you will get all the fluid out and damage in the system will become pretty easy to feel.

If everything feels ok hook everything back up and put new fluid back in. I always use new fluid.

This stuff is cheap and it can get overheated and burned. Old fluid will also have small metal shavings or metal particles floating around in it.

Power steering fluid acts as much as a lubricant as it does hydraulic oil. Keeping it clean and fresh will save you headaches on rebuilds.

Ball Joints and Spindles

Damaged ball joints are pretty easy to spot and are the most likely item to bend in a crash.

A bent ball joint can cause all sorts of steering problems which will seem like gremlins taking over your car. When I hear a driver complain about inconsistencies, the first place I look is the ball joints.

The easiest way to check ball joints, besides just looking at them, is to take the shocks and springs out of the car and let the front end hang free on jack stands. Steer the car back and forth. If the spindle moves up and down as you steer, you most likely have a bent ball joint.

It also helps to un-bolt the tie rods from the front end and just have the upper control arm, lower control arm and spindle hanging there as a unit.

Just steer it back and forth by hand. You'll easily see or feel the suspension move if there is a bent ball joint.

Sometimes the spindle can bend too. This is a little harder to detect.

Take the spindle off the car and look it over.

Turn it on end and look through the ball joint bores. Since these taper, they will look like concentric circles stacked evenly on top of each other. If the spindle is bent the ball joint bores won't line up from top to bottom.

Many companies also make spindle checkers which consists of two inserts which fit inside of the spindle bores and have the center drilled out to run a rod from bottom to top.

There are different ball joint tapers, so when ordering the checkers make sure you know what ball joints your car runs.

One area that many people, and even I myself, have ignored over the years has been the steering arm.

Years ago, if the steering arm got tweaked a little, we would just adjust the toe on that particular side and keep running it. If the steering arm got too bad, we would replace the spindle. For the most part, though, we'd give the tie rod a quarter or a half turn and keep running the spindle.

Then, a couple years ago, I really got investigating the front ends and Ackerman steering. Having the proper Ackerman in your front end can be a huge advantage. And, tweaked spindles can greatly affect the Ackermann. Now, unless I can figure the Ackermann didn't get affected by that bent spindle, it gets replaced.

When you start running tweaked steering arms, handling will start to degrade over time.

This is often a common scenario I see.

You'll have a great handling car.

Get into a crash.

Replace a bunch of stuff and adjust for the tweaked steering arm.

The car will still be ok, but maybe will have lost a little something. You'll adjust for it someplace else and keep racing.

A few weeks later you'll get into another crash and go through the same routine. Replace other parts and adjust for that bent steering arm.

Soon you'll have adjusted for that steering arm too many times and it's now way out of whack.

Your car has fallen off and you really don't know why.

Those small tweaks slowly caught up with you and now you've adjusted for them in so many other areas, you really don't know the way back to that original great handling car.

Spindles can be expensive, but I think they are essential to a good handling consistent car.

Checking Out the Rear End

Another often overlooked part of the car is the rear end. These things may look tough, but they actually can bend or develop problems after a crash rather easily.

One of the biggest areas is bent axle tubes or side bells.

Two of the most popular rear ends in the country are the Ford 9" and the quick change.

That's what I will concentrate on here.

There are other rear ends in use, but I have little experience with them, and to tell the truth, everything I'll be talking about will apply to almost any rear end with only small specific differences on how they are built.

On a side note, if your rules allow it, I would definitely run a quick-change rear end. I know there are some issues with drag and horse power loss by using them, but for the durability, ease of use, availability of quality parts, and cost, I think they can't be beat.

You may be able to get a little extra horse power, or save a little drag by using a Ford 9". To build a good one, that will hold up to higher horse power motors, will cost more in the long run than a good reliable quick change.

The cost of putting together a gear set with an aftermarket nodular iron case, good bearings and gears was approaching between $800 to $1,000.

That's creeping up to the cost of a quick change.

Here are some ups and downs to both rear ends.

First, you can get side bells in four, six, or eight rib versions. As of this writing, Winters has come out with a new eight rib bell which is extremely strong.

For a modified especially, this is the route I would go.

We even have gone to these bells on the late models I work on.

There's a problem I've been noticing for a couple of years now and I'm going to take a little time and describe some things to keep an eye on.

This may not be the most appropriate section, but since we are talking about rear ends, now is as good of time as any.

First, the use of brake floaters and the tendency to ride the brakes to "keep the car up on the bars" is taking its toll on the rear end.

Riding the brakes, while you are on the gas, is like giving your car more traction than you've ever had in your life.

It takes less torque and horse power to break the car loose on the track than it does to spin the tires when you applying the brakes. Running the brakes and the gas at the same time can cause quite a bit of damage to drive line components.

Let's think about where the stress is inside a rear end. You are taking something that is spinning in one direction and trying to spin it in another direction.

This happens with the ring and pinion.

Quick Change Problems

On a quick-change rear end the ring gear is on the left side of the pinion gear.

As torque is applied to the rear end, it tries to separate the ring gear and the pinion. The bearing race that supports the ring gear against the pinion is in the side bell. With excessive traction, or applying the brakes, the pinion tries to push the ring gear out the left side of the rear end.

This can cause side bells to break or if a weak four rib side bell is used, the bell can stretch and cause excess back lash. This excessive backlash can cause pitting in the gear set and eventually start breaking teeth.

Most rear ends include an inspection plug in the right rear side bell.

With a good flash light, you can see into the rear end to check the gear set.

After a hard crash or even as routine maintenance, take the plug out of the side bell and check for pitting or missing teeth.

Once a year the rear end should be taken apart and bearings and races checked for wear.

I you ever brake a drive shaft, there is a good chance the lower shaft and yolk could be bent.

I've spent a lot of time in the past looking for a mysterious vibration after a broken driveshaft only to find out weeks later it was either a bent lower shaft, bad lower shaft bearings, a bent yolk, or even broken bearings in the back cover.

Now, these items are the first thing I check after a broken driveshaft.

The final side note I must talk about is that the rear end really needs a good breather. The heat expansion inside the rear end can cause havoc with seals.

Breathing the rear end is a must in my eyes.

Ford 9" Problems

The Ford 9" is a little different.

The same problems can still exist.

On a quick change the pinion is in the center of the ring gear so the stress is a little different. It pushes directly in the center of the ring gear.

On a Ford 9" the pinion is below the center line of the ring gear, so the pinion has to climb the ring gear as well as trying to separate itself from the pinion.

The main problems I've seen occur on Ford differentials is the breaking of the ring gear caps and the breaking of the case.

If they are set up properly, I haven't seen too many problems other than broken cases or blown out caps. All the failed gears or bearings I've seen have come from failed cases.

In recent years, we've been updating our Ford gear sets to nodular iron or after-market cases. These are sturdier than the stock Ford case. With the increase in traction over the years, by better understanding suspensions and shocks in particular, stock cases just don't hold up.

This unfortunately has pushed the cost of the Ford gear sets between $800 to $1,000. It really is good that modifieds now have moved to quick changes. It will save everyone money in the long run.

Hubs and Axles

Hub bearings need to be packed occasionally. Depending on how often you race, I recommend about three times a year. Sometimes if you just pop the caps off the hubs you can see if there is a problem starting to arise.

What you are generally looking for is that there is still solid grease packed in the pockets between rollers. Make sure it's still the color it was when you put it in there.

This means it's not burned from overheating or has been mixed with dirt or water.

You should also check the preload on the bearings.

I've heard of (and used once in a while) the torque number of 26 ft. / lbs. for hub bearings.

Some people think this is too much.

I think it's a little different torqueing a freshly packed bearing rather than re-torqueing a bearing that has been run.

After a bearing has been run for even the bare minimum for a couple laps, re-torqueing to 26 ft. / lbs. might be a little excessive.

After a couple of laps have been put on bearings, enough grease has been pounded out of them that torque may cause excessive heat and drag.

I do believe though that 26 ft. / lbs. might be totally ideal for a freshly packed new bearing without any laps on it.

The one maintenance item I do check every race without fail is the tightness of drive hubs.

It seems many manufacturers under design these and they will loosen up almost every week. Especially on late models.

I used to insist on eight bolt versions, but everyone screams for lightweight over durability. Eight bot flanges have pretty much gone by the wayside.

Now, five bolt versions are the norm and they need to be checked every race night.

Axles don't require much maintenance. I always recommend getting the best axle possible. And, as of this writing, Strange Engineering has the best.

I do recommend installing them with a good quality lubricant on the threads. Joe Gibbs Driven Oil makes a spline lube that seems really good. I've always used a very thick anti-seize to do the job if spline lube isn't available.

At bare minimum, you need to use something to keep the axle splines from grinding away at their mating surface.

Many people like grease. I just don't think it has the lasting power to keep friction off the splines.

I prefer the specialized spline lube or a very thick copper anti-seize.

Greasing Your Car

Make sure everything that has a grease fitting gets grease often. Common items are ball joints, rack and pinions, birdcages, bell housing idler gears, and, sometimes, transmission tail shaft housings.

Let's talk about ball joints a little.

First, I like keeping ball joints greased. Pumping grease into ball joints will help keep them clean.

Dirt is the biggest killer to a race car besides concrete walls. Always try to keep things as clean as possible.

Howe ball joints are precision machined and will work better when freshly greased. Fresh grease will create a hydraulic wedge inside the ball joint.

Try pulling the grease gun line off of a freshly greased ball joint. Eventually, as the car runs, the grease will get pounded out from inside the ball joint. For a brief time, the cars suspension will be floating on a cushion of grease.

The latest fad in birdcages is roller bearing.

These are pretty much maintenance free except an occasional check over for wear and tear or breakage. There are some grease able birdcages still for sale. They are generally cheaper than bearing birdcages.

Here are the problems I see with grease-able bird cages.

First, they are not friendly to side load.

Some use nylon washers and some use brass or bronze washers to try and take away binding on side load. Whatever you use, you still need a favorable gap in the side slop of the birdcage to eliminate as much stiction as possible.

Second, dirt is an abrasive. Even if you are very diligent with maintaining you grease able birdcages. Aluminum tubes can get ground away and scarred by the continual grinding of dirt between the tube and the cage.

Maybe a steel tube will be more resilient to abrasion, but you will have the same stiction and side load problems.

Weekly Motor Maintenance

I've been told by a major dirt late model motor builder that dirt is probably the biggest enemy for motors. So, the most important thing you can do for good motor maintenance is keeping everything clean.

This starts with filters.

There are basically two general classes of filters used in racing that I am aware of. They are paper media and cotton or clothe media; disposable or rechargeable. There are very good arguments for both. I'm going to tell you everything I know about both.

Which are better?

You need to make your own decision.

First, from what I understand, paper media will filter better, but will restrict more.

Cloth media filters, like the popular K&N filters, is more porous and there for needs help to keep the dirt out. K&N uses an oil for this purpose.

They claim they can be recharged by soaking in a soapy solution to release the dirt as well as some of the oil. Then, the spray on oil is reapplied and the filter is ready to reuse.

Paper media filters are not reusable. You just throw them away after every race; Or, at most, after two races. It depends on the amount of dust produced at the tracks you race.

I've used both over the years.

Right now, we are currently using K&N's and recharging them a handful of times before either throwing them away or selling them to other teams.

Some motor builders suggest using K&N's twice without recharging and throwing them away. They claim a racer can never get them clean enough or the dirt gets so embedded you'll never get it out.

I have this philosophy. When the money you saved on recharging a K&N reaches what you would have spent on putting a paper filter on every night, toss it and start fresh.

You just broke even on your filter.

And, you used something that seems to flow better than the cheaper paper media.

Oh, and don't forget to clean those valve cover breathers every week.

Since you need to take them off when washing your car anyway, throw them in the soaking tub and then re-oil them before putting them back on.

Valve cover breathers can be a major point of entry for dirt into your motor.

Other maintenance I routinely do on motors is checking valve lash, checking belts, changing oil, cleaning and lubricating the carburetor checking all your fluid levels, and checking timing.

Your motor builder can give you guidance on all of these, so I will not go into great detail.

I do have one other thing I think is often over looked or not given enough time on each week. Something you really need to be diligent on.

That is flushing the radiator.

A plugged radiator is the number one problem I've seen when a car starts overheating.

I flush the radiator extremely well every week.

Every two to three weeks, depending on how dusty the tracks are, take the radiator out and flush it really well.

It takes extra time. But, I've seen more motors lost by overheating due to a plugged radiator than anything.

I also recommend running a very high pressure radiator cap.

I don't really see a downside to running a high-pressure cap as long as your hoses and radiator can take the extra pressure.

This means running a racing radiator and hoses designed to run at higher pressures.

Putting water under more pressure will raise the boiling point and help prevent overheating. Run as much pressure as your equipment will allow. Check with your motor builder for their recommendations.

Keep the radiator clean and keep the fins from restricting air flow.

Second, keep the battery charged.

Most dirt cars I know don't run alternators. You really need to keep the battery at full charge especially if you run other accessories like fans or blowers.

Engine ignition systems like voltage. The voltage will begin to drop as the battery gets weak. Your motor will start running bad. Especially under sever traction loads.

It's not a good thing.

Charge the battery as often as possible; even at the track if you have the means.

Lights and Electrical

While we are on the subject of electrical issues, I usually take a couple of minutes and give the lights and electrical a little check.

I'm going to get a little off tangent here while we are on the subject of electrical wiring.

Do you wire your starter push button so it's constantly live?

It probably is a good idea.

Spinning your motor over before flipping the ignition switch is a very good idea.

First, it's easier on the motor to start it after it is already turning it over. Especially if you are running a locked advance on your ignition.

I also have some experience with cracked bell housings when not spinning the motor over before starting.

If you are running a reverse mount starter with an idler gear, like a Bert or Brinn, there is a tremendous amount of torque being fed back through the starter and bell housing.

If the motor back fires even a little, it forces the torque back through the starter and can break the starter housing and bellhousing.

I've seen many cracked bell housings before discovering the problem was not spinning over the motor before flipping the switch.

If you are installing a new prewired ignition panel, you may need to swap the leads on the switches to make this happen because most are wired to only supply power to the push button after the switch is "on".

I usually just switch the markings on the wires and route them accordingly.

I also recommend using led light bulbs if the gauges don't come with them.

Especially if you are running a 16-volt battery and ignition system.

The 16-volt system will shorten the life of a typical filament bulb. Plus, as a bonus, they are brighter.

I'm really getting to be a fan of LED lights in general.

I know some people who have installed them on the back of their trailers for work lights. They are awesome bright. They amount of light they throw really makes a difference.

We also started using them as work lights around the car.

We used to use those halogen work lights.

Man, I hated them. You'd brush up against them and get burned.

They were fragile. One little bounce and they would break. What a pain. Do yourself a favor and get LED.

Hauler and Trailer Maintenance

Our trailers and haulers often see the least amount of maintenance and are one of the most important tools to the race team. We always just rely on them to be ready to go. Being stranded on the side of the road with problems is a real pain.

Depending on the type of hubs you have, I like to pack wheel bearings once or twice a year.

Some hubs have what they call "easy grease". This is a spindle end which has a grease zerk on it.

Just plug the grease gun on the end and fill them up. I don't know if I trust these as much as a standard packable bearing.

I've seen "easy grease" bearings fail.

One particular team I know swore they would grease them every other week.

When one of their hubs failed, I looked at it and it appeared as though it had never been greased.

There is also something called oil bath hubs. These are usually only on the heavier axles.

Axles designed for 8,000 lbs. and above.

These seem to work well.

Just keep an eye on the oil level. And, take them off once a year to flush them out and fill them back up with fresh oil. The oil in the hubs gets dirty and burned just like any other oil.

This all really depends on the number of miles you put on. I usually do them in conjunction with checking the brakes.

Speaking of brakes, this is another item that really needs normal maintenance.

Failed trailer and / or hauler brakes can get pretty scary when you're trucking down the road, something happens, and you can't stop.

You can usually feel brake problems start to develop as you drive. For good measure, I suggest at least once a year taking everything apart for a visual inspection.

I usually do this in the fall before everything goes away for the winter.

It seems in the spring, it's too hectic getting everything else ready. Brakes usually get over looked.

I've saved the lights for last.

Lighting and electrical problems can be one of the most nerve-racking pain in the neck problems on a trailer.

A short or bad ground can sometimes take hours to find. They should be checked though, before you head out every time.

Body Work and Cosmetic Crash Damage

I usually put this somewhere near the bottom of the list of things to do for the week. Aerodynamics are pretty important, but I've seen some pretty banged up race cars win races. It really doesn't get higher than this on my list.

Beside I hate dong it.

I make sure the wheels aren't obstructed by bashed in body panels, the suspension is free to move, and nothing is dragging the ground.

This seems to be a common problem with late models. As soon as the nose gets damaged it will really upset the car. This is usually where I start with my crash repair.

Since the nose is trying to blast a hole in the air for the rest of the car to fit through, it is really the most critical to keep right.

You want the nose to prevent as much air from getting inside the car. This means getting the nose as close to the ground as possible without touching it.

Once the nose starts digging in, it will take grip off the front tires and add drag to slow the car down. The hardest part to repairing a nose is the bumper.

The aluminum can be straightened with a dead blow plastic hammer or even a rubber mallet.

Just lay it on something hard and flat and start pounding away.

Bumpers are something else entirely different. It seems, once they get bent they are hard to straighten. If at all possible, I recommend straightening them without unbolting them from the car.

Once you unbolt a bent bumper it will be hard to get it straight and get it to fit back on the car. The best option, at that point, is to get something new.

Then you will know the nose will line back up. This will also insure your heights will be right as long as the mounts on the frame are straight.

Modifieds are a little easier. The bumpers aren't as critical because they aren't used to hold the front nose. These can get pounded around a little without having to worry about aero. Just make sure they don't get bent down and start digging into the track.

I would suggest building yourself a body kit. We have a little gardening tool box we bought from a garden center. This will have enough space to hold just about everything you'll need at the track or at the shop.

Here is a list of things I would recommend you put in your kit.

4" locking vise grip seamers. These are great for fixing folded parts that have been crushed in a crash. I use them to put hems and creases back in bent panels.

Rivets of assorted sizes. I like a multi grip length rivet. I opt for an aluminum rivet with a steel mandrel.

Just don't forget to pick up the rivet stems after they spit out of the back of the gun. These and tires don't get along too well. Oh, and get some aluminum back up washers too. Once the holes get over sized from drilling out old rivets you'll need to use these on the back side to pull everything tight again.

An assortment of body bolts. These are ¼" bolts with built in washers that were used to bolt body panels together on cars back in the sixties and seventies.

They still use the same style of bolt now, but they are usually metric. Allstar Performance or just about any racing supplier sells these in two different sizes.

They usually come in kits with ¼" serrated flange nuts. These are great on bodies. You don't even need a wrench for the back side. You can grip them with your fingers and tighten them until the serrated part digs in.

An air rivet gun and a hand riveter. Really the only thing you'll need the hand riveter for is to reassemble panels with different size rivets. Changing the little tips at the track when you are in a hurry will be a pain. I use the hand riveter for ⅛" rivets and the air riveter for 3/16". Ninety percent of what you will use will be 3/16" rivets.

Do yourself a favor and get an air riveter. The time you will save will be well worth the cost. Besides, they have come down in price over the years.

Now, you can pick one up pretty cheap.

I love welding clamps or squeeze clamps. I use these all the time when lining up panels to be re-riveted. You can clamp panels together to get a look at things before final assembly. An assortment of sizes and styles should be part of your tool kit.

A cordless rechargeable drill and plenty of spare drill bits. Cordless drills are pretty cheap nowadays.

When I started working on race cars they weren't as common. Then they were considered a luxury. I would get the best you can possible afford; get two; and get extra batteries charged and ready to go for when you need them.

For drill bits, get plenty of ⅛", 3/16", and ¼".

You will go through them like water.

For hammers, I like the plastic dead blow style. These won't damage aluminum panels. They seem to get them nice and flat. Some people like the rubber mallet style hammer for doing aluminum, but I've never had too much luck with it.

A nice ball-peen hammer will come in pretty handy and I like a 4-pound maul hammer for straightening the stubborn steel parts.

And, last on my list is somewhat of a luxury item. It is a ⅜" drive cordless impact. We nicknamed these a zippy wrench. They aren't essential, but they are nice for quickly assembling bolted body panels.

We have two.

One always has a 7/16" socket on it so it is ready for quick body repairs. They've come down in price and will save you a ton of time on body repairs.

Oh, I almost forgot.

A tool which I love.

It's custom made.

It is a steel backing plate used for pounding panels flat that are still mounted on the car. A friend of mine used a ⅜" steel plate that is roughly 5" x 8". and welded a little handle on it.

You can hold it in one hand on the back side of a panel and pound the panel flat.

That's just a basic list of things we use. Over time you'll discover tools you like and add them your collection. I always say tools are never a bad investment if they will save you time or eliminate frustration.

Shock Maintenance

I think shocks are often one of the most over looked maintenance items on the car. As long as they are bolted on the car people just leave them be. But, a bound-up shock can throw your entire car off.

The first thing to do is pull the shocks off the car every week and degrease them. Then, you can get down to business checking them out. Just keeping them clean will prevent suspension problems and shock problems in particular.

Push them in and out to make sure there is no obvious binds. Bent shafts or dented bodies are some of the most common things to look for. Twin tube shocks can take a little more abuse to the body before they start to bind.

Mono tube shocks are a lot less forgiving of body damage. I've seen some very minor scraping on the body create a bind in the shock. Sometimes a small amount of scraping will create just enough of a flat spot to bind the piston.

Inspect the shafts. If you see any scrape marks, this could indicate some other suspension problem going on. Scrape marks on shaft usually mean that at some point the shaft is seeing some huge amount of side load.

This can come from running a very soft spring at that corner and it is bowing. The bowing of a coil over spring will cause a side load to be put on the shock shaft. This can also become a major problem if the shock is often running at full extension. The support from the rod guide and the support from the piston are too close together. Any slop in either are greatly amplified and the shaft will push at an angle into the shock.

This'd load can show up as galling on the shafts, if they are too soft, or worse it can scrape the piston or the inside of the body of the shock. The internal gouging can be twice as bad and undetectable without taking the shock apart.

It really depends on the shock manufacture, but what will eventually start happening is the rod guide on the end of the shock body will begin to ware out and oil will start to leak out of the shock.

Shock manufacturers have been trying to reduce drag in the rod guides for the last couple of years and they seem more prone to damage and wearing out. To make them lower drag, they also made them a little sloppier and not as forgiving of wear.

Also, look for nicks or burs on the shafts. These are seal wreckers. Damaged shafts need to be replaced as soon as possible. But, if you are in a bind you can take a file and some very fine sand paper and work the nick down.

This is definitely not a fix because the shaft and more than likely the seal is already junk, but this will get you by one night if you are in a pinch.

It really depends on how much oil has already leaked out of the shock. If you feel a dead spot when moving it in and out it's already too late.

Too much fluid has been lost and you need to get it fixed before running it again. At this point it will only hurt the performance of the car.

Another area that I see needs almost constant attention are the rod ends.

It seems these are bound up on almost every shock I get in for service. The biggest problem I see is on aluminum shocks.

If the aluminum alloy they are made from is too soft, they will distort and bind from just normal running. This doesn't happen with all shock brands, but there are a couple I continually see problems with.

You also need to watch the type of cleaners and lubricants you use. Many cleaners and lubes will swell Teflon causing it to bind worse. I like plain old WD-40 or Tri-Flow for lubricating shock eyes and rod ends. Cleaning them with just soap and water will get rid of many problems without doing any damage what so ever.

Here is a little trick I may get some heat over, but it seems to work.

Just don't go overboard.

For those rod ends that are bound up from being distorted, I use a small hammer and tap them back into shape.

If the outer housing is aluminum and the inner race and ball are steel, you can usually tap them back round by tapping on the opposite side of the bind.

I don't suggest going overboard on this. Whaling on your shock with a hammer is not a proper fix. But tapping it back into shape by using the back of a vise as an anvil can take the bind out if you are in a pinch.

If your shocks are rebuildable, I do recommend a rebuild once a year. The oil inside will get dirty and burned.

Material from the piston band and walls of the shock get embedded in the oil and this stuff will change color and seem to get thicker.

A good disassembly and cleaning once a year is all they should really need. If you are constantly running long races or they are always running on really rough tracks where they are seeing very high amounts of heat, they may need servicing more often.

A good rule of thumb, though, is once a year.

The only other thing I recommend is keeping the dirt scraper clean. This is the top seal you see where the shaft enters the shock.

This also seems to be a big area of neglect and can add quite a bit of drag to the shock. I lubricate this often with a little WD-40 even when I dyno shocks.

Washing Everything Up

It's probably strange to see this section this far down on the list, since it is the first thing we do on a normal preparation week. But, the fact is, if you are in a bind for time or help on a particular week, this is the least important.

Like I said, this is usually the first thing we do after race night. Usually the next day, when we roll everything out of the trailer, it gets washed before it gets put away or gets worked on.

I am somewhat particular about washing. I really hate doing it. But, it is something that needs to be done.

We take as much time washing the suspension and the underside as we do the body.

The car goes on jack stands and the tires, fender, hood, and any other removable panels come off.

Next, we spray on the degreaser and let it soak.

There is a little point of contention among racers. Some say to use a pressure washer; others a garden hose. I like them both.

I think there are some places where water shouldn't go. I limit pressure washing to once every two or three weeks.

When I do use a pressure washer, I avoid things like brake calipers, starters, and ignition units. (distributors and MSD boxes)

It is real important to keep tires clean. Dirt will actually draw the oils out of a tire and make them harder. You will want to keep your tires clean. The cleaner you keep them the longer they will last.

Rubber is really a unique animal. It actually has a shelf life almost like food. Sunlight and ozone will start to harden and degrade the rubber. We really need to keep the rubber as clean and supple as possible.

Keep our tires out of the sunlight the best you can. If you have an open trailer, the tires are often exposed to the sunlight. They are on the tire racks baking in the sunlight to and from the races.

I have seen guys put tires in the back of the pick-up truck bed and put a tarp on them to keep them out of the light.

Another thing you might already be familiar with is grinding tires.

If you are new to the sport you might actually not understand why we do it. Or, why it's so important.

A tire hardens from outside to the inside. The outside of the tire will actually grow a callous on it like your skin. Grinding the tire will take the callous off and expose the soft supple rubber underneath.

Since rubber starts to harden as soon as it's exposed to sunlight and air, the closer we can grind the tires to race time the better.

To get back to the original discussion, tires need to be washed after every race weekend to keep them a supple and fresh as possible. This is one of the only areas I think a pressure washer needs to be used every time you wash.

A heated pressure washer is the best way I know of getting all the dirt out of the pores of the rubber.

We always try to blow off the carburetor and anything that has gotten onto the ignition. We also run the engine and bring it up to temperature to try and dry everything out.

A word of caution here. There will be water left in the radiator fins. Blow the radiator fin section out well with air before starting the car. If you don't, the fan will pull all the water out and it can get fed right into the carburetor. Plus, it will make a mess of the rest of the car.

The final process I need to talk about after a pretty thorough wash is getting it dry.

We have really hard water by us, so we like to towel dry with some old towels. After putting in all the hard work it's tough to stand back and look at a car with a bunch of water spots. It takes an extra two minutes to towel dry it and it's really nice to stand back and look at a shiny clean car.

Additional Must Do's

There are a couple of extra things I do from week to week to keep everything running smoothly. The list laid out for you may seem pretty daunting, but if you have a little help and you're organized it will go pretty easy.

One thing you will have to do every week is replenish your stock of either parts or what I call consumables that you've used the week before.

By consumables, I mean stuff like paper towels, brake cleaner (the handiest stuff you use on your race car), brake fluid, fuel, tear-offs, etc.

Everybody has their own way of keeping track of what parts they go through and what they need to order.

I have a dry erase grease board in the trailer. I jot notes down throughout the weekend. Then Monday morning I go over the board and figure out what I need to order.

I do usually like to get all my parts ordering done Monday morning. If any of the parts you will need for the next weekend end is backordered, you will have time to put together a plan to get what you need someplace else. Or, borrow one from another racer.

We trying to go racing week to week. Many times, your largest obstacle will be just getting the parts you need in time.

It seems like racer time is always, "I need it now!".

Manufacturers time or retail store time is, "We'll get it when we get it."

Both never seem to jive.

Save yourself some headaches and start ordering parts and making a plan on Monday. Or, as early in the week as you can.

The last part in this section I want to talk about is solving handling issues. And, were to start with your car going into the next race weekend.

I'm not going to get into specific handling changes.

I've written another book for that.

I will write other books about that.

I write a blog and newsletter about that.

This section will be strictly the mind set I use to go about prepping your car to go to the track.

First, often times you will make handling changes to your car throughout the night to accommodate changing track conditions.

If you are racing the same track every week and you are comfortable with your base line set up, don't forget to undo what was done at the track.

I see and hear about so many racers that forget to return their car to its starting setup point. Then, they go out and the car is either too tight or too loose.

I use the grease board in the trailer to write down changes. Or, I go over the notes we take throughout the night. We keep track of all the adjustments we make in a note book.

I just use those notes to back track the adjustments and get the car back to its baseline.

Or, what I have done in some cases is make the notes right on the car. I use white pieces of duct tape on the frame and write on these with a Sharpie Marker.

This is usually only as a reminder of where the wheelbase is at or if we turn on the spring screw jacks. Quick notes on the frame like this are nice to jog your memory if you are looking for a particular handling change.

For instance, we may roll the right rear wheel base back two turns and decide to leave it there for a couple of weeks as we experiment with other things.

We may, at some point, forget that the right rear is rolled back.

The tape notes on the frame are a quick reminder when we are struggling with a loose car.

As you race, you will develop your own system that will work for you.

Chapter 9
Setup and Car Handling

I need to preempt this section by telling you upfront that I will not be able to give you the ideal setup you will need to win races.

There are so many different classes. So many different types of cars.

There is no way I could tell you everything about every type of car in the confines of this book.

Car setup will depend on two factors.

The car and the driver.

The crew may be able to help along the way by giving some insight. Maybe, doing some work to alleviate some of the work.

But, ultimately it will come down to the driver and the car.

The driver needs to know how he or she needs to make the car feel so they can win races.

The driver needs to have the instinct and the knowledge to know whether to change their car of change their driving to get the most out of the car.

I've seen cars which are race winners and record holders in one drivers hands. Only to then finish last in another.

The second driver then makes a couple changes to the car and even more changes to their driving, just to put the car back up front.

I see too much speed lost in driving when the set-up of the car is blamed.

Racing is a combination of the two.

I will use this section to define some terms, explain the basics, and give you a couple of tricks I've learned along my thirty-year journey in working on these cars.

Ready?

Let's get started.

The first this thing you will have to decide is where to get some help.

Sometimes, you will get lucky and find a crew member or two working on or setting up the type of car you'll choose to race.

If this is not the case, maybe you could find someone and pay them to help you out a little.

Here is the biggest thing about racing.

To get good, you will need a lot of track time and practice. The more you struggle with an ill handling car, the longer it will take you to get good.

Just learning the basics from someone who knows your type of car will put you way ahead of the curve.

Even if you are on a budget, the best money you can spend is to pay someone to help you get started.

I've seen deals for cash.

I've seen deals setup for a steak dinner in trade for a little time explaining things in the shop.

The hardest part is finding someone reliable to get you started on the right path.

I would ask around at the track you want to run if there is anyone who's willing to give some advice or setup your car for the first time.

When selecting that person, I would steer clear of anyone claiming to have the magic setup. I'll tell you right now it doesn't exist.

What you need to start is a car that will steer good, be easy to drive, and adapting to different track is rather simple to understand.

If you can't understand the changes you will make to the car, you will have a hard time determining when and when not to make the change.

Sound right?

Let me give you a little analogy.

Let's say someone tells you to soften the right front spring and take some compression out or the right front shock when the track dies out.

I know this will take out dynamic wedge more quickly and make the car tighter on entry off the gas.

As a new racer, if you don't know what this does.

And, your car is already too tight on entry, this will hurt you even more than help.

I've seen a bunch of people give advice like this without explanation of what it will actually do.

Or, they never even ask how the handles in the first place.

They just dole out information based on what they would do rather than what the car actually needs.

It's a shame too many racers get lead down the 'magic trick' path from the beginning. Too much time is wasted trying to get a good understanding of how their car reacts to changes.

Only take advise from people willing to tell you 'Why', 'When, 'What'.

Why you want to do what you want to do.

When (under what conditions) to do what they are telling you to do.

What it does to the car to make the best desired effect.

If these people can't answer these questions I might look for someone else to lead you.

They may be knowledgeable. But, you need to understand more about the changes you are making.

Let's talk about the best ideas to get up to speed quickly.

Racing Schools

I've been to a number of racing schools and seminars thought my years. Some good.

Some not as good.

But, none were ever bad.

Anytime you have an opportunity to learn, the better. Even if it's just a little of a refresher.

The best course I ever took was three ten hour days. Taught by a Formula One engineer.

The least favorable one was by a fellow chassis builder who used it more as a selling platform rather than a learning platform; even though we all paid to be there.

I always take away something I can use to give the cars I work on just a little bit more of an edge. Sometimes it's just by planting a seed of an idea for me to explore on my own.

None were a waste of time or money.

The nice thing about the internet is everyone is online now advertising their seminar.

Find a website (local or national) which caters to the type of car you are racing. Start browsing or asking on a forum where you can find a good racing school.

Forums are also great places to get feedback from previous attendees. Ask around and find out if the course you are considering gets thumbs up by other people.

I think as time goes on the racing world will catch up with technology and you will start to see more courses and education online for racing people to enjoy in the comfort of their own homes over the internet.

I kind of see a future where a seminar could be taught in real time over the internet where attendees could interact with the teacher, ask questions and get instant feedback; just like they as if they were in a regular classroom.

Another way to get the help you need is to setup a deal with a local car builder.

Chassis Builders

Look around at the track you will be running. See who is fast.

Look to see who is building those fast cars.

Contact that builder and see if they have any help programs. Many builders have used cars to sell. These cars can either be 'trade in's' or house cars that the manufacturer put together to test or promote their own products.

Either way, these are usually fast, well maintained cars. And, chassis manufacturers are usually more willing to help you with your learning curve to get you up to speed and make their cars look like magic.

At the very least, if you buy a car from a manufacturer, negotiate an initial set up and scaling. This will at least insure you will be on the same page with their current thinking and not years behind the curve.

In certain areas of racing, technology moves very fast. Starting out on the leading edge through a manufacturer will at least get you on the right path from the start.

Also, find out what their policy is on continuing help. The mindset is this.

If you buy a used car from a manufacturer you are already on their radar. You have already spent money with them. They know you want and need the help.

If you buy a car used from a third party. You have not spent any money with the builder. They really don't know the condition of the car you bought. They are not familiar with you at all.

Getting their best information or them taking a ton of time with you will be tough. They may give you their basic setup, but may not be inclined to spend a ton of time with you or give you their best information.

All that being said.

Let's dig in and set down some basics to how a car handles. I'll give you some basic guide lines to start your journey into the racing world.

There will be some basic tools you will need to set up your car and help you measure where it is at.

Wheel Scales

These are not necessary to buy, at least not at first. These are a large investment and you can probably get by for your first couple years without them. You can usually either borrow some, rent some, or try to find someone to help you out who has some.

Unless you have a large initial budget, I would steer clear buying a set right off the bat.

When you do decide to finally buy a set, I have some recommendations.

First, I believe the traditional gain scales to be the best. There are some problems with electronic scales. To make them affordable enough to sell in the field of racing, the load cells used are not on the high end.

They use what is call an 'S beam' load cell; as opposed to a pancake load cell. Basically, it is a piece of steel shaped like an 'S' with a kind of stress strip called a strain gauge attached like tape to the side. This measures deflection and the computer inside converts it to the proper weight load.

The problem with this is when you start introducing side loads through wheel scrub. This can start to create inaccuracies.

I've built platform risers with steel ball transfer on the bottom to try and take the bind out of the system, but this is very dangerous and I don't recommend anyone try this.

When I did it I had a car hoist set up to catch the car in case it slipped off the scale pads. It does work, but I would never have attempted this without the hoist as a safety protection.

The car has, on occasion, come sliding off the scale pads only to be caught by the hoist.

If the hoist wouldn't have caught the car, I would have been crushed.

Another safety precaution I always take is to always scale the car with the driver. When on the scale pads, the driver holds the brakes to lock the car in place.

I've heard too many stories of people getting crushed by cars. I don't take any chances.

Please always think ahead to keep yourself safe.

I also heard there is sometimes a problem with humidity. Humidity can cause electronic components to corrode. As they corrode, the resistance values change and this can create a percentage of error.

I'm also not a fan of electronic scales because of the wires leading to the wheel pads.

If you do get in the market for electronic scales, I'd recommend getting the ones that are wireless and communicate with the computer readout box through radio frequency.

The real problem with these is that you need to keep the batteries fresh. As the batteries start to go bad the values will start to change.

I've chased my tail several times making adjustments to the car only to find a bad battery and having to start over.

Caster, Camber, Toe, Ackerman, Bumpsteer

These are what I call the core fundamentals of front end alignment.

There are other things that go into front end design, but if you are aware of these, you will have a pretty good head start.

Caster

Let's begin our discussion on front end alignment with caster. This is the leaning of the center line of the spindle front to back when looking at it in side view.

Picture walking up to your car from the side and looking at the wheel.

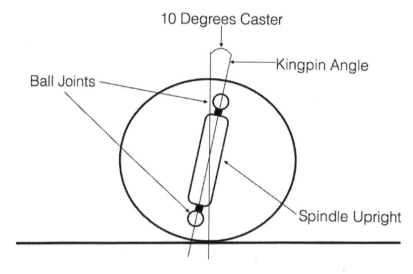

10 Degrees Caster

Kingpin Angle

Ball Joints

Spindle Upright

You spindle, or wheel upright as some people call it, is what your wheel bolts to that connects your top and bottom control arm.

If the point where the spindle bolts to the upper control arm is more toward the rear of the car than where the bottom control arm bolts to the bottom of the spindle, that wheel is said to have positive caster.

If the top is closer to the front than the bottom, it is said to have negative camber.

You will need to get a caster / camber gauge. These are not too expensive.

The newest and greatest are digital, but I'm not sure you really need a digital one.

These gauges work by sweeping the spindle in both directions and measuring the change.

There are some different ones out there, but the ones I have used the procedure goes like this.

Turn the front of the wheel out twenty degrees. Set the adjustable bubble to zero. Then, turn the wheel so the front is in and read the bubble.

To clarify what I mean by in and out; when checking the right front wheel, out is right turn and in is left turn. For the left front tire, out is left turn and in is right turn.

If you do this backward or you are not accurate the twenty degrees, your measurement will be off.

I have seen gauges whose procedure is different so make sure you read the instruction that come with the gauge.

As far as determining how far to sweep the twenty degrees, many of these gauges have the corners of the gauge cut at twenty degrees.

If the frame rails of your car run parallel to the center line of the chassis, you can judge the twenty-degree angle by holding a straight edge up and measuring the front and back to the frame rail.

When I'm in a pinch I have just guesstimated the twenty degrees and have been pretty close. It really depends on your threshold for accuracy.

The most accurate way to get the twenty-degree sweep is to use a set of turn plates. These are a set of plates your front wheels set on with degree markings on them. Between the two plates are a set of bearings.

As you turn the wheels the plates swivel to tell you the degrees you front wheels are turned.

Turn plates are also a handy way to determine the amount of ackermann steering your front end has built into it. This is not the tools I use to determine ackermann, but I've known some people who do.

I use a different method and I'll go into more depth on that subject when I get to that section.

So, what should the caster be? It's all kind of subjective and it really depends on several other factors that are built into your car, track shape, and driving style.

First of all, let me explain what caster does. Positive caster will add a stability to the front end of the car.

Think about a caster on the front of a shopping cart. (this example eluded me for years because people were so used to giving it as an example I don't think they thought through exactly what was going on)

A shopping cart typically has negative caster. The top of the pivot was ahead of the bottom of the pivot.

Have you ever noticed, especially on those old steel frame shopping carts, that if they had no weight on them and you pushed them around, the front wheels would just flop around and wobble?

Negative caster has the least resistance and least stability. Those carts would turn on a dime and the caster would always want to find the negative position.

Spin the cart around and the caster would spin to find the negative position.

The neat thing about negative caster is that you could steer the cart rather easily no matter how much weight the cart had piled on it.

The front of the shopping cart would spin effortlessly making it easier to steer just off of the rear wheels.

Race cars generally use positive caster. This adds stability to the front. Remember how the caster on a shopping cart would just flop around when it had no weight on it? Your race car with positive caster will not tend to do this. The more positive caster, the more stable.

The problem with too much caster is that it will make the car harder to steer. (the opposite of our loaded shopping cart) That's why years ago it was always suggested in order to run excessive amounts of caster you needed to run power steering.

I don't think there are too many race cars that don't run power steering any more. That kind of went away in the eighties and nineties.

I do know some race cars that are built to run negative caster on the left and positive on the right. Which brings me to my next topic on caster.

Caster Split

For circle track cars, who only turn left, it is common to run more positive cater on the left than on the right. This will make it easier to turn the car into the corner.

The left front is less stable and wants to turn easier than the right. If the left front has two degrees of positive caster and the right has four, the car has two degrees of split.

If the left front has one degree of negative split and the right has two degrees of positive caster. The car has four degrees of split.

How much split and total caster do you need?

It really depends on a bunch of other settings and the way the car is built.

Here is the list:
1. Whether your car has power steering. This is usually not an issue any more, but remember, the more positive caster the car has the more of a strain it will put on the power steering system. Some of the more modern steering systems are tunable to feel. If your car has more caster, you may need to run a softer servo or torsion bar in your servo to help you steer without getting too fatigued in long races.
2. How much toe you want to run. Toe can also have a stabilizing effect to the front end. If you are running a minimum of toe, you may need a little more caster to keep the front-end stable. And, vice versa.

3. Speed of the overall steering system. Some steering systems can get pretty fast. Small amounts of hand movement can have a big effect on the cars steering. This is a combination of the speed of the rack or box and the steering arm length. If the steering gets too fast, it may seem to be unstable or wander down the straight. Adding caster can make this a little more stable. Or slowing down the steering and taking away caster might be better.
4. This can be one of those tuning options I was talking about.

I would work with your car builder on some of this stuff before changing settings drastically. Some car builders design stuff to act a certain way.

Altering these settings may upset the balance of the car. Sometimes it is better to change the speed of a rack or box, or torsion bar or servo, rather than altering the front-end settings. Although, by knowing what your changing and why may lead you to a much better handling car.

Now let's talk a little about camber.

Camber

Camber is the leaning of the top of the tire away or toward the centerline of the car.

When the top of the tire is leaning toward the center line of the car, that tire has negative camber.

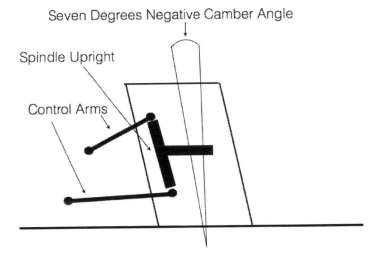

Seven Degrees Negative Camber Angle

Spindle Upright

Control Arms

Right Front Tire Viewed From Back

If the top of the tire is leaning away from the center line of the car it has positive camber.

Camber adds traction to the tire by equalizing the pressure across the tread surface. The amount of camber you need is largely determined by the construction of the tire.

A dirt late model tire will require different camber than a dirt modified tire, a street stock tire, or even a stock production street tire run in on a four-cylinder car.

But, static camber settings don't always tell you the entire story. We'll talk more about this in a little while.

First, let me explain a little how camber actually works to get you the most traction out of the tire.

As you travel through the corner the tire will hold the car in the line you choose from sliding across the track. We'll call this side bite.

You will have side bite on both the front and rear of the car.

The more load you put on that tire to keep the car from sliding, the more the tire will stretch and deform. Kind of like a rubber band stretching.

To understand this thought a little better we'll use a rubber band as an example.

Take a rubber band and lay it flat on the table. Put your finger at one end of the loop and put pressure on it to hold it in place on the table.

With the other hand, stretch the opposite end of the loop. If you don't increase the pressure on your finger holding the band, at some point the rubber band will reach it's limit and start to slide across the table.

To hold the one end in place you will need to add more pressure to your finger or make the rubber band stickier so it won't slide.

Adding camber is like making the rubber band stickier.

Now let's look at how a tire can get stickier to the ground as you are running it.

A tire is a lot like a rubber band because the wheel is rigidly mounted to the car (your finger) and the other side of the tire is in contact to the racing surface (the table).

The tire is stretched just like in the above example. A tire filled with air will stretch more than a solid rubber tire like on a wagon or tricycle.

The more it stretches, the less load gets put on the inside of the tire and the more load gets put on the outside of the tire. If one part of the tire has less load on it, it won't be as sticky as the part with more load.

We call the portion in contact with the track surface the contact patch. A lot of people think that the contact patch is all the same. As long as it is in contact with the road, it's fine.

I think the patch can actually have different loads across the surface, so there is more to it than meets the eye.

To cure the problem of the inside having less load than the outside, we put camber in the tire. This will put more initial load on the inside when the car is sitting still.

The idea is to equalize the load across the tire when the tire is at its maximum effort to hold the car from sliding sideways in the middle of the corner.

The camber it needs to equalize the pressure depends on the deformation of the tire due to load. It also depends on how the tire is constructed.

Softer sidewalls and lower air pressure will generally tend to need more camber. But, this won't always hold true because there will be a certain amount of camber gain built into the car.

The length and angle of the suspension linkages will produce a gain in camber as the car rolls. The more gain in camber, the less static camber the tire will need to equalize the pressure across the contact patch.

I won't get into how this really all works. That is the topic for a different more extensive book. I'm just trying to keep it simple here.

There has been a trend lately toward excessive camber in the front ends on dirt cars. I started asking the question about why people are doing this because if you look at tire wear patterns on the tire, the amount of camber is not really justified.

Then I started looking at other things excessive camber can produce.

I go into slip angle and slip ratio a little further in the chapter, but I will give you the quick version so we are on the same page with our discussion.

Go back and think about our rubber band example. If you take your finger off the part of the rubber band that is pinching it to the table, the rubber band will snap back into place.

As your tire rotates, there is always an amount of rubber that is going into the contact patch and a certain amount that is leaving the contact patch.

The part leaving the rear of the contact patch is snapping back into position.

This action provides a shove in the direction the top of the tire is pointed. This is kind of the same theory of how slip angle works to help turn the car.

As you turn either left or right, the contact patch is twisted a different number of degrees than the wheel and spindle on the car. The snapping realignment of the rubber is what helps turn the car.

That is why when the car is tight, all you need to do is turn the front tires a little further and the car will begin to turn. This is just putting a little more slip angle into the tires.

Toe

To fully understand one of the often overlooked and hidden gems of speed in the racing world, we need to fully understand toe.

Look at your car from the top down. Notice that, in most cases, the front of the tires, as a pair are pointed toward the outside of the car. Hook a tape measure in the center of one of the front tires and string it across the car and measure to the center of the other front tire, you will notice the measurement will be larger than doing the same measurement in the rear of the tires. This is considered "toe'd out" the amount of the difference.

Put this another way. Stand up and look at your feet. If your toes are pointed away from each other, you are "toe'd out". If they are pointed toward each other, you are "toe'd in".

Toe will add stability to the car by adding a scrub. Both front tires pointed out a little bit puts tension on the front end and makes the car track steady.

A car which is "toe'd" in will tend to wander and be unstable. The rule of thumb is to always make sure that your car is always toe'd out. Most common measurement is ¼" to ½".

Now on to the hidden gem. This is one of the most misunderstood and often overlooked front end adjustments you can make.

Ackermann

Ackermann is when one tire turns more than the other when steering left or right. Normally the inside tire should steer further.

This comes from the old western days when they had wagon wheels made out of wood.

For each wheel to turn independently, one wheel will scrub more than the other. With wooden wheels, the added scrub would break the center out of the wheels. So, Ackermann was created to keep the scrub to a minimum and keep the front wheels from breaking out.

Let's think about how this actually works.

First, think about a car at the center of a turn. Let's keep our thinking to just standard street cars. At the center of a corner, draw an imaginary line through the rear axle or the center of the rear wheels towards the center of rotation of the car in the turn.

Now, draw another line through the center of each of the front wheels, perpendicular to the way they are pointing. If the inside tire is turned more than the outside, there will be a point where the front tire lines will intersect.

This will eliminate the scrub out of the front end of the car. Now, if you can get all three lines to intersect at a certain point, the scrub will be totally eliminated from the entire car. The car will rotate around that point without any bind.

If the inside tire turns more than the outside tire, the car will be "toe out" as it turns. And, it can toe out a very large amount in some cases.

If the inside tire turns less than the outside tire, the car will be "toe in" as it turns. There is a major problem if the car 'toe's in', especially under counter steer. I've heard a 'toe in' Ackermann car will feel darty and unpredictable.

It's kind of strange. Everyone is worried about checking toe, which is a static car state measurement, but no one wants to check Ackermann.

Ackermann is probably just as important or even more important than just checking toe.

So, what happens on a dirt car that not only turns left, but also spends a certain amount of time turning right to counter steer and keep the car from spinning out.

170

If you turn right into a counter steer, the car will begin to toe out and add a substantial amount of scrub to the car. Picture a car with one inch or better of toe. That car will be extremely stable, but there will be a large amount of scrub which will reduce traction and reduce acceleration off the corner.

I've heard drivers explain this to feel like there being a parachute hooked on the back of the car.

For a typical dirt track car now I set Ackermann to be zero in counter steer and left turn to be as close to ¾" to 1" toe'd out at full lock left. This helps traction and acceleration off the corner. Then, the large amount of Ackermann turning left will help the car turn into the corner.

Now let's look at some basic car alignment.

Wheel Alignment

I believe one of the most important things you need to concentrate on is the wheel alignment. This can make or break a car.

There are many things that mask themselves as other problems; when actually they are wheel alignment problems.

Let's think about how wheel alignment actually works to tighten or loosen your car.

If you stand at the back of your car and sight down the tires, you will probably notice the front being wider than the rear. This adds tightness and stability to your car. The rear end will want to resist sliding.

But, that is if you want to go in a straight line. What if you want to turn or straighten yourself out after you turn?

Putting any one of the rear tires outside of the front tires will help the car turn the car in the opposite direction.

Put the right rear tire outside of the right front tire and the car will want to turn left. Put the left rear tire outside of the left front tire and the car will want to turn right.

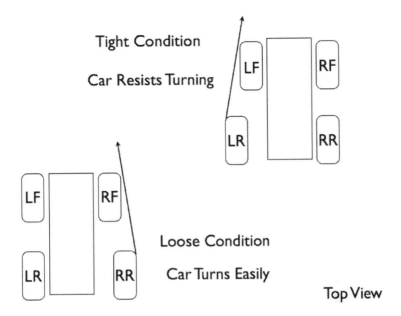

Tight Condition

Car Resists Turning

LF RF
LR RR

Loose Condition

Car Turns Easily

Top View

Here are some easy to follow guidelines for circle track cars, but the same will apply to road course cars. You just need to do the opposite when right turns are involved.

If your car is loose coming off the corner, putting a wheel spacer on the left rear will tighten your car up.

If your car is tight going into the corner, putting a wheel spacer on the right rear will loosen your car up.

If your car is loose going into the corner, moving your right rear tire in will tighten you up.

I don't know many circle track cars that are really good where the right-side tires aren't within an inch or two of lining up. Some people who drive modern four link race cars (dirt late models and dirt modifieds) will say that the offset between the right rear and the right front is greater than one inch.

Well, statically it is, but if you look at the car in a dynamic state, you will see a different story.

A four-link car will have a really large amount of rear axle loose steer. As the left rear is pulled ahead, the right rear is pointed toward the right front. Now, with that amount of axle steer, you will need to counter steer the front tires to get the car to track straight on the straightaway.

Now, if you were to string a car in this dynamic state, you would notice that the right-side tires come even closer to lining up.

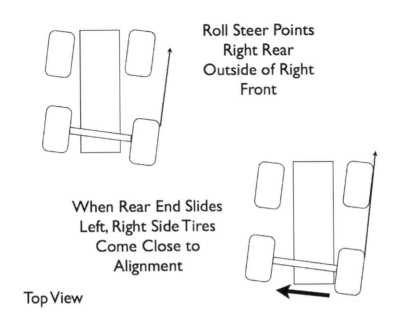

Roll Steer Points
Right Rear
Outside of Right
Front

When Rear End Slides
Left, Right Side Tires
Come Close to
Alignment

Top View

How does a panhard bar effect this situation? A panhard bar locates the rear axle laterally in the car. Sprint cars use a panhard bar in the front to locate the front axle.

One side attaches to the frame and the other side attaches to the rear end. Exactly where it attaches and the height of both attaching points will have an effect on how your rear axle will line up in a dynamic state.

Panhard Bars

A common panhard bar among dirt track racers is what they call a "J" bar.

Most of the time, it attaches to the frame on the left and wraps over the top of the pinion mount to attach to the rear end on the right.

Usually the vertical split in the mounting points is between eight and ten inches.

As the car rolls to the right, the left side frame mount is raised even higher than the rear end mount. The rear end is then pulled left further in the chassis.

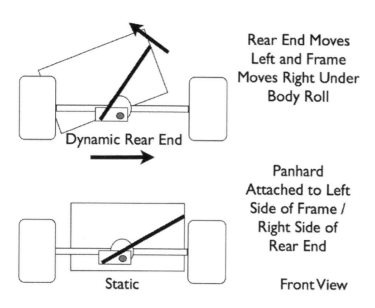

Rear End Moves Left and Frame Moves Right Under Body Roll

Dynamic Rear End

Panhard Attached to Left Side of Frame / Right Side of Rear End

Static

Front View

This will get the right-side tire to line up even closer than before.

If you think about everything working in a circle or on an arc, you can see how this works.

The longer the "J" bar, the less the rear end is pulled left and the looser the car will be.

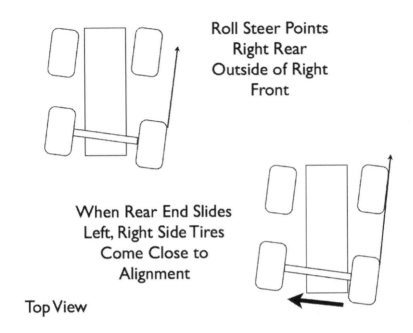

Roll Steer Points
Right Rear
Outside of Right
Front

When Rear End Slides
Left, Right Side Tires
Come Close to
Alignment

Top View

The more angle (the larger the split between mounting points), the further left the rear end is pulled; the tighter the car.

I get asked questions all the time about what different panhard bars do and how different splits effects the car.

Just keep the above idea in mind and you will be able to figure out any different panhard bar arrangement.

Another aspect to panhard bar angles that needs to be kept in mind is the angle which they are mounted effects the side load on the right rear tire.

Very basically, the more the angle, the more it pushes down on the right rear tire; making the car tighter.

The mounting height of the bar on the rear end and on the frame in relation to the ground also makes a difference. I get into that in more detail in my racing secrets book.

Let's talk a little about the panhard bar, or 'track' bar, commonly found on asphalt cars throughout the country. If you've ever watched a NASCAR race on T.V., you've probably heard the commentators talk about teams adjusting the track bar throughout the race.

They often use the track bar to tighten or loosen the car depending on what they need the rear end to do.

These bars are commonly mounted on the right side of the chassis and the left side of the rear end; often times on the left side axle tube.

If the frame side is higher than the rear end side, the rear end is pulled left under body roll. This pushes the right-side tire further under the car and the left tire further outside of the left front tire. This can cause the car to be tighter in many applications.

This is taking into account that you are continually lengthening or shortening the panhard bar to keep the tires in the same alignment statically.

Under NASCAR pit stops they do not have the ability to lengthen or shorten the panhard bar when the adjust height, so in affect the are statically pulling the rear end left to right in the car under yellow; as well as raising or lowering the roll center,

Raising the panhard bar in this instance will slide the rear end right and make the car a little looser. Lowering the panhard bar will in affect push the rear end left and make the car tighter.

The key element here is knowing where your panhard bar is located and how it effects rear end movement on the arc.

Weight and Weight Transfer

Weight distribution and where it transfers to under dynamic situations will be one of the biggest obstacles you will face with your car.

It's mainly because, without data acquisition or some other means of measuring this, it will be hard to determine what weight will do dynamically.

We do have some systems, but it will not be as accurate as having an accelerometer in the car.

First we need to understand static distribution before we can really dig into where the weight will go dynamically.

If you are running an oval track car, your left side percentage will be higher than the right. This is because weight will transfer to the right when turning left. Pretty self-explanatory.

This is where it gets to be kind of a balancing game. We want enough transfer in the rear to get the rear tires to equal in weight load. This will give you the best traction off the corner.

On a typical dirt circle track car, the left side percentage will be 54 to 56 percent of the total weight of the car.

I will run through how we determine this a little later in the book when we talk about 'scaling' the car.

For typical asphalt circle track car, people will try to get the left side as high as they can.

Most sanctioning bodies have now put a limit on the amount of left side percentage. Rules usually dictate something around 58 percent, but it varies for different tracks and sanctioning bodies.

If you are running road course cars where you are turning both left and right, the idea is to have the left side and right balanced as close as possible.

Well, this isn't entirely true. Many people will determine the layout of the track and devise a strategy centered around the cars balance.

Here is the best way I can explain this.

Let's say the road course is a one-minute track.

It's laid out so there are more and faster left hand turns.

There will be an advantage to get through the left hand turns better than the right.

If the car is set up with a little more left side percentage to get through the faster corners better than the competition, you will have an advantage.

You will find that so much in racing is strategy and out thinking your competition.

It's like a chess game. You will need to take into consideration everything you do.

One move will affect several other aspects on how you race.

Rear percentage is also something you will need to keep track of when setting up your car.

Unless you will be running a front wheel drive car, this will determine where much of your traction will come from.

This will also vary quite a bit from class to class and even from track to track.

If you have any friends or maybe even your chassis builder will be able to give you a good starting setup for a particular track you will be racing.

For your typical dirt stock car, you will need to have a good amount of rear percentage to get traction off of the corner. I usually see rear percentages in the 54 to 58 percent range of the cars total weight; although I have seen some higher.

For asphalt circle track cars, I have heard the range is closer to 51 to 54 percent. Because of naturally having more traction than dirt, the rear percentage doesn't naturally be as high.

The more rear percentage will make the car really tight (resist turning with the steering wheel). On the other hand, I've heard rear percentages as low as 49 percent. But, get too low and your car will be really loose (turns too easily and can cause the rear end to 'slide out' in the turn).

Setting up a car for a road course is much the same as the thinking that goes into asphalt oval cars.

If the course is small and has tight turns, where acceleration is not as important, then less rear percentage may be more beneficial.

On a course with long straights and tight turns, traction off the corner might be beneficial to beating the competition into the next turn; a little higher rear percentage might be necessary.

Diagonal is another aspect you will need to understand, but we'll get to that a little later.

Let's start focusing on weight transfer or where the weight will go as you drive around the track.

The best way I heard it described was at a chassis school years ago by a guy named Mark Busch.

He said that to keep it simple we really need to think of weight transferring only two ways. Front to back and side to side. There is actually a third dimension called yaw (rotational front to rear) but, for sake of simplicity we'll only talk about the two here.

Weight will transfer from the back to the front under deceleration and braking. And, front to rear under acceleration.

When turning left, weight will transfer from left to right. Or, if you are running a road course, weight will also transfer from right to left when turning right.

Springs don't effect the amount of total weight transfer, but they will determine where it will go and be an indicator of how much.

Because two things will rarely appear to happen independently, if you turn left and decelerate, weight will look like it transfers from the left rear to the right front. When you begin to understand how springs work, you will see how this weight transferring diagonally will only confuse you.

This is where we need to start understanding wedge or diagonal.

Wedge / Diagonal

Dirt oval track racers typically use wedge as their terminology. Asphalt circle track racers prefer to use the diagonal term. They are closely related, but not completely the same.

When you talk about wedge you typically are only talking about the rear tires. The wedge is the difference between the left and right rear.

If your left rear tire weighs 720 lbs. and you right rear weighs 600 lbs., you have 120 lbs. of wedge.

Diagonal is measured in percentage. It is the percentage of the total weight of the car that is on the combined right front tire and the left rear tire.

For example, the total weight of your car is 2300 lbs.

The left rear weighs 720 lbs.

The right rear weighs 600 lbs.

The left front weighs 500 lbs.

And, the right front weighs 480 lbs.

The combined weight of the right front and left rear is 1200 lbs.

Divide 1200 lbs. by the total weight of the car (2300 lbs.) and you get 52 percent.

The diagonal of that car is 52 percent.

While we're at it, the same math is used to find the left and rear percentages.

The left side total weight is 1220 lbs.

Divide that by the total weight of 2300 lbs. and you get 53 percent left.

The total weight of the rear tires are 1320 lbs.

Divide that by 2300 lbs. and you get 57.4 percent rear percentage.

Most common electronic scales do the math for you, but it is good to know where the numbers come from.

If you are using my preferred method of scaling your car with grain scales, you will need to do the math every time you make a change.

Let's get back to understanding why wedge is important.
Weight transfers from left to right and from rear to front under deceleration. To get a proper balance you will need to have the left rear tire be the heaviest on the car.

It will need to be heavier than the right rear. A too heavy of a right rear will resist the car from turning.

Picture sticking a rod through your car from the top down. Your car will turn and pivot around that rod. The right rear will want to 'skid' as the front pulls the car in the direction you want to go.

Engineers call this imaginary rod the yaw center. The closer to the front your yaw center is, the more the right rear will need to 'skid' to turn the car.

If your yaw center is closer to the rear, the less 'skidding' the rear of your car will have to do to turn.

To loosen your car up enough to 'skid' the rear the proper amount, you will need to add wedge to keep side bite out and allow it to turn.

So, when decelerating entering the corner, the biggest looser of weight will be the left rear wheel. The biggest gainer is the right front.

Typically, the more wedge or diagonal you run, the tighter your car will be on the gas and the looser your car will be off the gas.

Higher wedge or more diagonal cars will be tighter on acceleration out of the corner.

Now let's take a look at some basic rules of thumb of the last important major area of traction.

Traction

Traction starts and ends where the tire meets the road. The tire is at the core of traction.

Loading a tire more will always add more traction, but there is a point of diminishing returns.

If you look at a tire loading chart, a tire will start to fall off when it reaches a certain point.

Typically, a tire needs to stretch in order to provide the ultimate amount of traction. A tire can only stretch so far before it reaches the limit and starts to lose traction.

This limit is expressed in either it's slip ratio or it's slip angle. Slip angle refers to the sideways traction of the tire and slip ratio refers to forward traction.

Slip Ratio

If you look at a drag racing tire under slow motion as it leaves the line, you will notice a bulge at the front of the tire where it meets the track.

This bulge is created because the tire wants to push the car forward faster than it's currently moving.

The rubber on the tire contact patch is stretched as it enters the point where it meets the road and snaps back into place in the back of the tire.

This snapping motion is what propels the car forward. The tire needs to stretch to get the most amount of traction.

This is similar to the action we talked about with the camber in the front tires.

If a tire starts to bounce, the stretch comes out of the tire and it loses traction.

This is why we use springs and shocks in cars. Shocks help make a comfortable ride. But, more importantly, helps us get the most traction from a tire.

Exactly how shocks work is beyond the scope of this book. To fully understand this, you will need to get into a world of spring and suspension frequencies.

In the end of this book I have put together a list of references to help continue you your journey down the racing educational path.

What is really important here is the fact that you need to always think in terms of how your adjustments effect the tire contact patch and how the rest of the tire is stretched.

The other aspect of tire stretching has to do with side bite and how a tire is used to steer the car.

Slip Angle

Slip angle is the term used to describe how a tire actually turns your car. Just like slip ratio, it uses stretch to create traction and 'push the front end into a turning motion.

As your front tires are turned, the car and contact patch want to continue to go in a straight line. The hub and wheel of the tire are turned at an angle different than the path of the car.

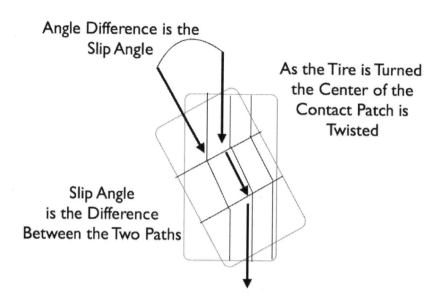

Angle Difference is the Slip Angle

As the Tire is Turned the Center of the Contact Patch is Twisted

Slip Angle is the Difference Between the Two Paths

The angle difference between the wheel when it's turned and the ground underneath, is the slip angle.

It's a similar action to what happens in the tire on acceleration.

The tire is rolled into the contact patch at one angle, is twisted where it hits the road, and then is snapped back into place as it leaves contact with the road.

This continuous twisting and snapping back into place as the tire rotates is what actually propels the car to turn; or resist turning when thinking about it in terms of side bite.

So, why is this important to understand?

I mean, just as long as your car turns when you turn the steering wheel, all is good; right?

Well, understanding the basic principles will go a long way into helping you solve handling problems with your car.

Let's think about it this way for a moment. If your car is perfectly balanced, you should only need to turn the front tires a certain amount to get your car to turn.

If your car gets tight and resists turning, you will need to turn the front tires more and increase slip angle to get your car to turn.

This will increase the snapping motion of the tire back into place and apply more force to change the direction of the car.

Every tire type manufactured has a different slip angle they can run at before the reach their maximum output. Once that maximum is reached, the tire will begin to skid.

The goal is to use the least amount of slip angle to turn the car as needed. The rest of the sideways stretch of the tire can be used as side bite of the tire.

Traction Circle

The tire only has so much stretch to be used. The more side stretch for side bite in the rear, the less stretch available to be used for forward bite.

The more slip angle used to turn a tight car in the front, the less stretch is available for side bit in the front.

Your car is just a series of tradeoffs.

The more side bite you demand of your car; the less forward bite your car will give you.

Your tire has only so much to give.

Great drives understand this either literally or intuitively.

If they crave a lot of forward traction when exiting the turn, they make sure not to get their car too tight and are using too much of the stretch in the tire for side bite. They know they will need it to be there for forward traction.

They turn their car early, or back up their apex of the turn, just so their car is pointed straight off the turn for maximum forward traction.

This is best understood by looking at an old concept of a traction circle.

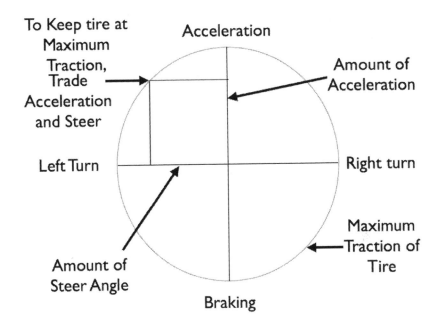

You are doing different things with your car at different points on the track. Sometimes you are braking, sometimes you are turning, and sometimes you are accelerating.

Your tire is providing its utmost amount of traction when it's on the line of the circle.

If the tire has more traction to give you, your traction demand will be plotted somewhere inside the circle. If you are demanding more from your tire than it will give you, you will be running it outside of the circle.

The goal is to always run your tire somewhere on the line of the circle or as close as you can to it.

If you use so much of the traction of your tire for braking, you won't have as much left for turning the car.

If you use too much for turning your car, you won't have as much left for acceleration.

Your race strategy needs to be centered around this balance of traction. And, you then need to setup your car based on your strategy.

Let me restate this because it is so important and racing your car, and this entire book rotates around this idea.

Racing is a strategy and a series of tradeoffs.

Tuning and driving your car around these limiting tradeoffs is the key to winning.

Chapter 10
Stringing Your Car

One section I really think is important for a beginning racer to understand is how to string your car.

This is something I wrote about in my other book and I thought I would just add it to the end here for your use.

This is something that should be done for almost any type of race car which races on any type of surface.

Knowing where your wheels align is critical if you race on asphalt. Small variations of even an 1/8" to 1/4" can make a huge difference.

First, you need to make sure both front and rear tires a squared up to the center line of the car. If your frame rails run square to the centerline of the car, you can simply place a straight edge on the sidewall of the tire and measure to the frame rail in front and in back of the tire.

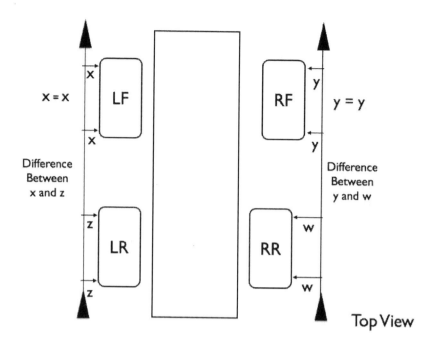

Top View

I use a straight edge on the sidewall and measure in front and behind the tire. When these measurements are the same, the tire is square to the center line. I usually clamp the steering shaft at this point to make sure it doesn't move.

The same goes for the rear. You need to know where your rear end is set in the car. I always try to get the rear end square; at least initially.

Next, I get some jack stands and some string. Place the jack stands ahead and behind the tires and run the string between them. The string will run along both sides of the car, parallel to the center line.

Measure from the string to the front and back sidewall of the front tires. Move the rear jack stands until this measurement is equal.

Now measure the distance from the string to the sidewall of the rear tires. This will show you where your rear end is in relation to the front tires.

Now if you want to get creative and start learning about where your wheel offsets move to dynamically, jack up the left side of the car and reset your jack stands.

This time, square the jack stands to the sidewalls of the rear tires. Turn your front tires until they are parallel to the string and this will show, approximately, how your wheel offset changes dynamically.

Where should your car be? Every builder has their own ideas, but it seems the most common is to line up the left side statically. The important thing is where everything runs at dynamically.

Well, now is time for some fun. Dig in and start experimenting with this stuff to learn as much as you can about your car.

Chapter 11
Conclusion

I really have to acknowledge some references that I used to build this book. These are not copied or plagiarized, but the concepts came from them and they deserve a plug.

I would like to say thanks to Tony Woodward for his great product catalog. I've been using his bump steer diagrams for years to give me a quick reference when setting bump steer on cars. The catalog is also an excellent reference to steering systems and technical information on how all this stuff works. I'd highly recommend picking one up.

Second I would like to thank Claude Rouelle. I took his three-day intensive workshop back in, I believe 2005. It was by far the best and most comprehensive course about race car dynamics I've taken.

It is very technical and not slanted toward the dirt racing market, but I believe all race cars are created equal ... at least in principle.

Third I would like to reference some good books to continue your education. Some of these aren't cheap, but these are what I reference when I run into a problem I'm really stumped on.

Any of the Milliken books on vehicle dynamics

The Rowley Race Car Engineering book. This book coincides with the use of the Bill Mitchell geometry software ... also a great investment to figure out how your car works. I have it and love it.

If you really liked this book and you would like to give me a little feedback, you can visit my blog and leave your comments in

the comment form in the 'contact' section. My blog is located at:

http://hogantechnologies.com/

You can also sign up for my mailing list. From time to time I give away special freebies to only my list of subscribers.

For instance, my previous book I gave away to my list for free. If you would like to be a part of my Facebook community search for Hogan Technologies on Facebook and hit the 'Like' button.

This will keep you up to date on changing technologies or any new ideas which seem to be coming around in the world of racing technology.

Thanks

Be FAST!

Kevin Katzenberg

Made in the USA
Lexington, KY
08 January 2017